IN PRAISE OF WOMEN

In Praise of Women

A Christian Approach to Love, Marriage, and Equality

Robina and John W. Drakeford

HARPER & ROW, PUBLISHERS

SAN FRANCISCO

1817

Cambridge   London
Hagerstown   Mexico City
Philadelphia   São Paulo
New York   Sydney

FIRST EDITION

Designed by Jim Mennick

Library of Congress Cataloging in Publication Data

Drakeford, Robina.
  IN PRAISE OF WOMEN.
    Includes bibliographical references.
    1. Woman (Christian theology) 2. Marriage.
3. Bible. O.T. Proverbs XXXI, 10-31—Criticism,
interpretation, etc. I. Drakeford, John W.,
joint author. II. Title.
BT704.D68   261.8'357   79-3000
ISBN 0-06-062063-3

80 81 82 83 84 10 9 8 7 6 5 4 3 2 1

Dedicated to Betty Dilday

the first lady of Southwestern Seminary, whose "husband sits among the leaders at the city gate," whose winning personality, common touch, and enthusiastic spirit have caused many to praise women.

Contents

Preface

A news magazine recently published a "feminist alphabet" consisting of twenty-six statements presenting the liberated woman's creed. Many readers called it cute, original, and unusual, overlooking the fact that one of the most unusual acrostics ever put together concerned a woman and was written thousands of years ago. This ancient acrostic, sometimes called "the alphabet of wifely excellence," describes an ideal wife. Concluding the book of Proverbs, the last verses are a twenty-two-stanza poem, each verse of which commences with a Hebrew letter. The acrostic form is used several times in the Bible, most notably in Psalm 119 and portions of the book of Lamentations. Some Hebraists think this acrostic form was used as a mnemonic device. The alphabetical form may have aided Hebrew boys and girls in memorizing the ideas.

Unfortunately, the alphabetic form of the poem is lost in the translation from Hebrew to English. To transmit the sense, I have paraphrased each of the verses, beginning with successive letters of the Roman alphabet. It would be ideal if we could make the Roman letter the exact phonetic equivalent of the Hebrew letter, but this is not possible. In any case, there is an element of artificiality in using either alphabet; and because it is a mnemonic device, the dicussion of phonetic equivalence is rather academic. Another problem is the length of the alphabets. The Hebrew alphabet has only twenty-two letters; the Roman alphabet has twenty-six. Consequently, I use only the first twenty-two letters of the Roman alphabet.

In the family enrichment conferences I conduct almost every weekend, I note the very keen interest of women. Most of those buying literature at the book table are women; so it seemed appropriate to write a book for wives, who are frequently the key members of the family unit. This conclusion has led to an unusual feature of this book—contributions by my conference coworker and wife, Robina. Portions printed in italics are added by Robina in much the way she does it at the conferences. I find myself holding forth to the assembled company and note a light coming into Robina's eye, indicating a contribution about to be made. I do not always welcome these intrusions; in fact, I sometimes ignore her signals. However, once she has spoken, I realize she has brought a distinctive feminine perspective to the subject.

As you read the italicized segments, prepare for a change of pace—a reminiscence, a slightly different point of view, an exhortation from the wife who presides over our household. You will probably be interested in her comments and identify with her feminine angle on the situation.

In many ways reading what follows in this discussion of Proverbs 31 will be like eavesdropping on a husband and wife. My wife and I have discussed this passage on many occasions, me spending much time with different translations, commentaries, psychological theories, and counseling cases, she reminding me of something I have overlooked.

Welcome to our family circle. We hope you will enjoy reading the material as much as we have enjoyed preparing it.

JOHN W. DRAKEFORD

PROVERBS 31:10–31

The following is a paraphrase of Proverbs 31:10–31 using the English alphabet to form an acrostic as in the original Hebrew.

Hebrew
Alphabet

א   A good wife is difficult to find, but once discovered will become more precious than gems to her husband [v. 10].

ב   B ecause of her sterling character, her husband has complete confidence and trust in her, and she will completely satisfy his needs [v. 11].

ג   C onscious of the importance of a positive attitude in her relationships with her husband, she is resolved always to be a help rather than a hindrance to him [v. 12].

ד   D oing something for the pure joy of it, she searches for and busily spins wool and flax [v. 13].

ה   E ver seeking to provide a varied diet for her family, she purchases a variety of foods shipped in by importers [v. 14].

ו   F eeling concerned about her family, she rises early to prepare breakfast and plan the day's activities [v. 15].

ז   G oing to inspect a piece of land, she buys it and plants a vineyard [v. 16].

ח   H er life is characterized by energetic hard work [v. 17].

ט   I n all her buying she carefully compares the available good and watches for bargains [v. 18].

י   J udging the indigent to often be deserving, she works with her spindle to make clothes for them [v. 19].

כ   K nowing poor people need more than material gifts, she reaches out both hands and touches them to indicate her compassion [v. 20].

ל   L ooking ahead to the snowy days of winter, she has
      no fear, because she works hard in the summer
      and fall to sew scarlet clothes to keep her family
      warm in the winter months [v. 21].

מ   M astering the art of weaving, she makes pillows and
      mattresses for the home and beautiful clothes for
      herself [v. 22].

נ   N ot threatened by his wife's skills, her husband sits
      amongst the leaders at the city gate [v. 23].

ס   O perating a business, she sews beautiful belted gar-
      ments, whieh she sells to Phoenecian traders [v.
      24].

ע   P alpably strong and dignified, she laughs at the future
      [v. 25].

פ   Q uietly attentive, she makes a wise response always
      speaking with kindness [v. 26].

צ   R unning her household with efficiency, she shows the
      value of supervision and example [v. 27].

ק   S he receives commendation from her children and re-
      joices as they stand up and bless her [v. 28].

ר   T ribute comes from her husband; he says, "There are
      many fine women in the world, but you are the
      best of them all" [v. 29].

ש   U nimpressed by flattering talk and superficial beauty,
      she knows true values lie in a reverential trust in
      her creator [v. 30].

ת   V irtue is rewarded as she is praised for all her good
      works even by the leaders of the nation [v. 31].

CHAPTER 1

The Going Rate for Wives

 good wife is difficult to find, but once discovered will become more precious than gems to her husband.

Prov. 31:10

ALEPH

Like the overture to a beautiful symphony, which announces the theme, this tenth verse of Proverbs 31 announces the message of the third appendix to the book of Proverbs. It introduces the most laudatory passage about women to be found anywhere in the Old Testament. In many ways this appendix is out of keeping with the earlier chapters of Proberbs, where women are not always referred to in the most flattering manner. In other portions of the book women are described as rottenness in their husband's bones, and as quarrelsome, complaining, cranky, awkward, prickly people who drive their husbands to distraction. Even at the beginning of this particular chapter the mother is warning her royal son about women who might seduce him and says women are "the royal pathway to destruction" (Prov. 31:3).

Now comes a new note. Proverbs 31:10–31 portrays a wife and her work in an idealized manner that is unparalleled in biblical literature. Although the Old Testament is a bastion of masculine superiority, there is no equivalent passage extolling the virtues of man. So flattering is this description of a wife that when the passage was read to an American audience, one very sophisticated man commented that no woman could be that good.

The very existence of such a passage may be a tribute to the sagacity of a woman. The early chapters of the book of Proverbs are credited to King Solomon, Auger, or King Hezekiah; but this last chapter comes from the pen of King Lemuel of Nassa and concludes with the significant statement, "Taught to him at his mother's knee." Here was a woman, a mother, getting her message to the world through her family. The passage may indicate that although women were held in low esteem in Hebrew society, they exercised a pervasive influence within their family unit and through it on society.

Behind this verse is the idea that wives could be bought like any other salable commodity. As one Bible encyclopedia notes, "In marriage a woman was practically the chattel, the purchased possession and personal property of her husband who was her master."[1] The idea of women being marketable products has continued in many cultures, where they sometimes refer to "bride price," a statement of the going rate for buying desirable brides.

An even more demeaning aspect of acquiring a bride is the custom of the woman's family providing a dowry. The implication of a dowry is worse than the presupposition that wives can be purchased in that it suggests she is of so little value that someone has to be paid to take her off the family's hands. An aspiring husband receives a bonus or premium to sweeten the pot. In *Fiddler on the Roof,* when Tevye, the father, and Lazar, the butcher, discuss the possibility of the butcher marrying Tevye's daughter, Tzeital, Lazar reminds him Tzeital has no dowry. With a family in such an impecunious position, Tzeital may not have many opportunities of finding a husband.

The ABCs of being a good wife present a different idea about the value of a wife. Whereas in our day a man can secure his wealth by investment in bonds, securities, or certificates of deposit, in Solomon's time the most convenient way of keeping one's assets was to acquire precious gems. In this passage in Proverbs Solomon is saying a good wife is more valuable than any gems a wealthy man might acquire.

Wealth is a subject under constant consideration in the book of Proverbs, which mentions it on at least fifty occasions. Much of the discussion focuses on the dangers of wealth, and a typical statement is "Trust in money and down you go." A recent study of very wealthy people confirmed the negative correlation between wealth and a viable family life. A deficient family may produce fortune builders. Max Gunther in *The Very Rich and How They Got That Way* shows that more than half the successful wealthy men he studied had lost a parent through death or divorce early in life. Gunther speculates that a sense of family insecurity may have motivated the person to work and accumulate wealth as a protection against further blows and misfortunes.[2] Studies of wealthy people have shown many of them to be preoccupied with money-making activities. The men were often cold, uninvolved husbands and fathers. They were frequently emotional strangers to their children, to whom they gave gifts but not themselves.

Having acquired their wealth at the cost of their families, were they satisfied? The billionaire J. Paul Getty, although born into a wealthy family, was an entrepreneur in his own right and amassed a fortune. Business was his life. He reviewed his married life—married and divorced five times—and lamented, "I hate to be a failure, I hate and regret the failure of my marriages. I would gladly give all of my millions for just one lasting marital success."[3] Perhaps this was Getty's way of saying that if you can find a good wife, she is worth more than precious gems.

All this talk about the value of wives as a commodity to be purchased by the man reminds me that the role women play in establishing relationships has changed across the years and continues to change, with women becoming more active in the process. Nowhere is this truer than in America. When we first came to the United States, I could hardly believe what was happening when girls would call up my sons on the phone. Of course, John always says I believe all the girls are out to get my sons. When I was a girl, it was up to the boys to take the initiative. My mother constantly exhorted her daughters to be ladies, and apparently to her one of the hallmarks of being a lady was not being aggressive in relationships with boys. Mother frequently said, "Flee and he'll follow; follow and he'll flee."

We live in a society where marriage is not thought about as seriously as it was when I was a girl. Among Christians, particularly, divorce never seemed to be an option; and we looked for a prospective husband with more serious intent than do many people today. Then there was the courtship period. John and I "kept company" for seven years before we married. During this time we got to know each other. We visited each other's homes, which was a revelation for us both. I was one of seven and John was an only child. He could not believe all the things that went on in a large family. I am grateful we had this long courtship.

We married and I soon discovered my husband's commitment to helping people found a ready response within me. When we attended conferences, it was not long before a group of women would be gathered around me, telling me some of their most intimate problems. In one of his books, dedicated to me, John says, "To Robina, who practices the psychology I teach."

It seems appropriate to me to describe a woman as a precious jewel, as the passage from Proverbs does. Like a diamond, she has many facets that shine to guide her in her efforts to cope with domestic responsibilities while living a fulfilling life.

As remarkable as this ideal wife might have been, her modern counterpart is presented with many new potentialities for developing her skills and abilities. Even if she is "just a housewife," her services are of considerable value. One of the best studies on the actual value of a modern housewife was carried out by the Chase Manhattan Bank, which estimated the housewife with no outside responsibilities might spend as many as 99.6 hours per week at twelve jobs in the home, including laundress, cook, dishwasher, nurse, and seamstress. The study concluded that if these services were secured in the open market at 1972 prices, it would cost $257.33 per week to duplicate them.[4]

If a wife is as valuable as all this, we may have to take a closer look at her. It may be we have been taking too many things for granted for too long. In the following chapters we shall examine many of the facets that shine from this unusual jewel of a woman.

CHAPTER 2

Trust and Fulfillment

 ecause of her sterling character, her husband has complete confidence and trust in her, and she will completely satisfy his needs.

Prov. 31:11

BETH

The second verse of this ode of wifely excellence, commencing with the Hebrew letter beth, brings an entirely new perspective on the status of women as revealed in the book of Proverbs. Opening with a warning about the seductive woman, this chapter is apparently continuing the seductive female theme. Not only were the "ladies of the night" seen in this way, but also certain married women. An earlier chapter spells out the techniques of the unfaithful wife as she approaches a simple lad, "Let us take our fill of love until morning for my husband is away on a long trip" (Prov. 7:18–19).

In Proverbs 31:11 we meet a different woman. She is the type of wife a busy man needs. Her husband is a civic leader, constantly meeting with the other leaders of the town at the city gates. His civic involvement means he will spend many hours away from home, but he can attend to his responsibilities without worrying about his wife's activity. The original Hebrew means literally "his heart can be at rest." He need have no anxieties about his wife as he goes about his work. She has a sterling character; he can trust her.

JEALOUSY

A relationship between a husband and wife must be built on a basis of mutual trust. Lack of trust gives rise to jealousy, a malignant disease that can destroy a marriage.

A man I counseled certainly knew the torments of jealousy. When James and Wanda Harrison's third child entered school, it seemed the perfect time for Wanda to use her secretarial skills. With James's encouragement, she applied for and obtained a secretarial position. After a few difficult weeks, Wanda found herself enjoying every moment of her work and returning home in the evening bubbling over with stories of the day's happenings. When the executive vice-president offered her the position of his personal secretary, it seemed she had really arrived; and Wanda regaled James with the stories of Mr. Gorman's qualifications and achievements. Then came the evening when she arrived home to announce she was taking Mr. Gorman to the boss's banquet as her guest. James blew his stack and said "no way." He did not want his wife spending her evenings as well as her days with her boss.

After a long session in which both James and Wanda made some unfortunate statements to each other, they managed to sit down and sort out the situation. James was penitent: "I'm sorry. I said things I should never have let pass my lips. The problem is that I love you so much. I sometimes wish I didn't care for you as deeply as I do." This all sounds very convincing and not a little flattering to James for his depth of devotion to his wife, but is his jealousy really a deep love for another person? Not everybody sees it this way. Psychoanalyst Fenichel suggests, "The most jealous persons are those who are not able to love but feel the need of being loved."[1] Thus jealousy may indicate a person feeling inferior and needing to dominate another.

Possibly the most worrisome aspect of jealousy is its kinship to some of the abnormal emotional reactions that plague human personality. The paranoid reaction is characterized by suspicion, a state akin to jealousy. As Schiller puts it, "Oh jealousy thou magnifier of trifles." In the words of the Apocrypha, "The ear of jealousy heareth all things" (Wisdom of Solomon 1:10). Paranoia has been called the counterfeit of reason because, starting from a completely false premise, the paranoid person presents a carefully reasoned argument for his position. This is the attitude many jealous people demonstrate.

The very fact that this civic leader can trust his wife not only tells us about her fidelity but also indicates something about him, as is seen in the case of a client we shall call Patrick Jackson.

Mrs. Jackson, a motherly type of woman, knows her husband is a conscientious worker at his civil service job. He has always been a good breadwinner but not particularly attentive or affectionate to his wife. She never could recollect the exact time when it first started, but Mrs. Jackson gradually became aware that all her actions were under her husband's close scrutiny. When he arrived home in the evening, he would quiz her about what had happened during the course of day, where she had been, whom she had seen, what she had said.

Mrs. Jackson soon began to wonder if she had been reading too many Agatha Christie mysteries. She had a strange feeling she was being followed . . . by her husband. One night as she drove to the store she saw their second car, her husband at the wheel, following her. Entering the store, she saw him drive around the block, then park where he could keep her under observation. Returning home, she was no sooner in the house than he entered with a story about slipping down to see Keith Johnson's new power saw.

At last Mrs. Jackson could stand it no longer and after a stormy confrontation suggested they see a counselor. Mr. Jackson finally went, reluctantly. Fortunately, he liked Dr. Johnson, the counselor, and soon found himself sharing his perception of the situation. He knew his wife was running around on him. While he was at work, she was entertaining men; sometimes when he was home, she would slip off for a rendezvous. The counselor asked about proof. He had no proof, but Mr. Jackson knew what was going on. When her turn came with the counselor, Mrs. Jackson was hurt, distressed, and denied all her husband's accusations.

A breakthrough came when Mr. Jackson revealed he was having an affair. In the strange reasoning that sometimes characterizes people like Henry Jackson, he felt his wife must be involved in the same type of behavior as he. If *she* were deviant, he could justify his own behavior.

Jealousy here was symptomatic of his own deviance. The excessively jealous person may need to sit down and evaluate his or her own behavior. Guilt can cause aberrations in the thought processes.

In *The Vindictive Story of the Footsteps That Ran,* Dorothy L. Sayers tells how Lord Peter Wimsey solves the mystery of a murdered woman by producing evidence to show her husband was the culprit. His inimitable servant, Bunter, asked a pertinent question, "And what does your lordship take the man's motive to have been?" After pondering the question, Wimsey recalls his biblical reading of early days and suggests a verse from the Song of Solomon may explain it all: "Jealousy is cruel as the grave."

NEEDS

HIM: Darling, I love you. From the first moment I laid eyes on you I knew you were the one for me.

HER: And I love you. It seems as if you came into my life at just the right time. Ever since I met you, life has been different.

HIM: Sweetheart, will you marry me? If you will only say yes, my life will be complete. We'll settle down in a little cottage. We'll have roses around the door and babies on the floor. I'll never want another thing.

Maybe. But do not take this lovesick Romeo too literally. Once married with cottage, babies, and roses, he may have at least one, two, or, as Maslow suggests, five different categories of needs that will emerge. Pondering the forces within the human personality, psychologist Maslow came up with a basic idea, "Man is a perpetually wanting individual," and went on to postulate we have a whole series of needs. Once a set of needs has been satisfied, a new set immediately emerges.[2] As our diagram shows, living life is like climbing a set of stairs as new needs emerge. Superwife is conscious of her husband's needs. As Proverbs 31:11 says, "She will richly satisfy his needs"; and this chapter suggests the best place for needs' satisfaction is within the family.

The first level of need is physiological. Studies have shown people deprived of food can think of little else. As Maslow puts it, "Man shall not live by bread alone unless there is no bread."[3] The psychological

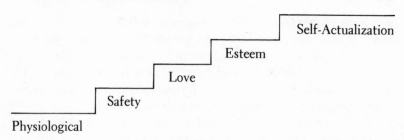

Physiological

need in a husband-wife relationship may take a number of forms. At the lowest level it is, of course, mere subsistence—food to eat and water to drink. The old saying, "the way to a man's heart is through his stomach," may be an unwitting confirmation of the truth of Maslow's theorizing. A wise woman who is to become a housewife will acquire at least a modicum of cooking skills and continue to develop an interest in the culinary art.

One very strange marriage was between the British politician Benjamin Disraeli and Mrs. Wyndham (Mary Ann Lewis). She was forty years of age; he was thirty. He was well educated, polished, and erudite; she never could remember whether the Greeks or the Romans came first, was talkative and tactless, and had unusual taste in furniture and clothing.

However, once married she became the ideal wife; and in the rough and tumble of British political life she was constantly at Disraeli's side and demonstrated her love for him by providing a home in the truest sense of the word. A debate in the House of Commons sometimes lasted until five in the morning; but Mary Ann would always wait up for her husband, the household ablaze with light to welcome him. She often waited outside the historic Parliament building in a carriage with a meal specially prepared for him. Mary Ann was vividly aware of the physical needs of home and food.

Significantly, Maslow considers sex a physiological need. Sex, like food, is a renewable pleasure that reminds men and women that they need each other. From our Christian perspective, we note sex is God's good gift to men and women and meant to provide us with some of our most pleasurable experiences. Although many of us are vividly aware of the necessity of fidelity to our partner, we may overlook our sexual obligation in marriage.

Early chapters in the book of Proverbs recognize sexual needs, the way they should be satisfied, and the role of a husband and wife. The writer presents the possibility that a man's sexual needs may cause him to turn to a prostitute for satisfaction. The interesting possibility of counteraction lies in a husband and wife both recognizing a spouse's sexual needs. "Let a young wife be your joy, a lovely hind, a charming doe is she; let her breasts give you rapture, let her love ever ravish you. Why be ravished with a loose creature and embrace the bosom of another woman?" (Prov. 5:18–20, MOFFAT). Here is counteraction, fighting fire with fire. God, who has planted the sex drive in humans, has also provided the means of satisfaction within a marriage, an experience that will surpass illicit sex.

Once a person's physical needs have been supplied, it might be imagined everything would be rosy; but survival and well-being are not ends in themselves. Maslow points out that a new set of needs becomes obvious and the individual wants to live in an orderly world. Maslow referred to these as safety needs.

It used to be said that an Englishman's home is his castle, a place he can feel secure from any possible attack from the outside world. It now turns out that the biggest threat may be from *within* the family. One magazine article set forth some disquieting facts, indicating family members are more physically cruel to each other than they are to unrelated individuals and acts of violence range all the way from slaps to murder.[4] One peculiar aspect of this is highlighted in the *New York Times,* which reports the number of people killed by relatives in a six-month period was greater than the number killed in three and a half years of political warfare in Northern Ireland. The article points out, "Almost all family violence, including everyday beating, slapping, kicking and throwing things is carried on by normal everyday Americans rather than deranged persons."[5]

Tragically, the family, which should provide experiences of intimacy, all too frequently teaches violence. The most potent teaching takes place through that most influential of all teachers, the TV set, where violence reigns supreme. Add to this the model presented when a parent loses his temper and attacks other family members, and you have a particularly difficult situation.

But this senseless use of violence is only one of the ways individual safety needs may be denied. The more subtle way is seen in a home where the family is at odds. In an apparently good family in which there is no physical violence, many threats may underline safety needs. Husbands and wives who periodically threaten to leave home, throw down the gauntlet to a spouse, or tell the children, "One afternoon you'll come home from school and I'll not be here," are effectively undermining safety needs.

Toffler has called the family the shock absorber of society. It is the place where people return after a bruising day in the outside world. If it is nothing more than a place of conflict and insecurity, it is failing to fulfill the all-important safety needs of individual family members.[6]

Security by itself is never enough. People in prisons are secure but they live very unsatisfactory lives. Whatever he may have misinformed us about Sigmund Freud certainly taught us men and women need to be loved. Studies across the years have shown that love is the one indispensable element in raising a baby and also later on in childhood. The family thus becomes the milieu within which love is received and given.

As important as is the receiving of love, it shrinks into insignificance in the total love experience; for the pathway is from self to others, from receiving to giving. Under the influence of love, the personality unfolds and expands. Then like the baby, who, having grown to adulthood begets children of his own, the mature person inevitably moves out from being loved to take initiative in loving and in turn providing for others what was so essential in his own experience.

Love is the most creative of all the emotions. Anger, envy, and resentment are primitive responses that are blindly and illogically bent on expressing hostility, leaving destruction in their wake. The great anatomist, John Hunter, is reputed to have said concerning his heart condition, "My life is at the mercy of any rascal who can make me angry."[7] Negative emotions, Samson-like, not only tear down the structure of human relationships but destroy the subject in the collapse. By contrast, the positive power of love brings out life's healing potential.

Because of its pervading power, love is the supreme activity of the human personality. Paul says, "whether there be prophecies, they shall fail; whether there be tongues, they shall cease; whether there be knowledge, it shall vanish away . . . love never fades" (1 Cor. 13:8). One by one the coveted gifts of ministry, prophecy, tongues, and knowledge will fulfill their purpose and cease to be; but love continues unabated as the immortal aspect of personality.

Agape or giving love has been expounded with great clarity by Pitirim A. Sorokin, whose personal experiences could hardly seem less likely to convince a man of the power altruistic love. A leading Russian intellectual, Sorokin was not sorry to see the overthrow of the backward Czarist regime and worked as secretary to Kerenski, the leader of the provisional government. After the Bolsheviks had displaced the elected representatives of the people by force of arms and assumed control, Sorokin became an object of their antagonism. Pursued and imprisoned, he lived in daily expectancy of death, watching his fellow prisoners taken away to be shot.

In the midst of all these horrors, Sorokin kept a diary. He concluded that his nightmarish experience had taught him three great lessons: First, life even at its worst and hardest was the most beautiful, wonderful, miraculous treasure in all the world. Second, the fulfillment of duty is the response that makes life happy. Third, it is utterly futile to try to create a new world through cruelty, hatred, violence, and injustice. The only way is through creative love not only preached but constantly practiced.[8]

It is small wonder Sorokin dedicated himself to the propagation of his idea of altruistic love. Shakespeare's description of mercy applies equally to love: It is twice blessed, blessed in those who receive and those who give.

At a time when the family is frequently ineffective, many concerned individuals are working diligently to provide services to help shore up this important unit of society. There is a multiplicity of services: child care programs to free the mother, breakfasts and lunches for children, education for all family members, and care for elderly parents to release the family from these responsibilities. One of the unfortunate results of all this activity has been that the family, relieved of these responsibilities, has become increasingly weak. Considering the deteriorated situation, a concerned family member is apt to point out how society has taken over family responsibilities and ask what is left for the family to do.

The answer is that the family does what no social service agency, or all-powerful welfare state, can ever possibly do—it loves. No impersonal agency or jaded social worker can ever fulfill this vital function. The family supremely loves.

Although much sentiment, almost maudlin at times, has been expressed about mother love, in the majority of cases the mother still sets the love level of her home. A distraught mother poured out the story of her son to a counselor. She concluded her pathetic tale with a question, "What shall I do?" The counselor gently took her hand and responded, "Mother, you go on doing what you've done in the past. You love him. When he falls, you'll be waiting to help him get to his feet again." The wife and mother is the pacesetter for the skills of loving. She provides the climate within which love needs are met.

On every individual's chest, invisible, of course, are inscribed the words, "I am of value." Every one of us needs to feel important; every person wants to march at the head of someone else's parade. Romantic love frequently develops on this basis. Two people look at each other and see qualities not obvious to anyone else, provoking the statement by people who know them, "I don't know what she sees in him." Of course you don't. She sees something no one else is aware of. Two kids in the throes of romantic love give all their attention to each other and in this obsession build a sense of self-importance that fulfills what Maslow calls their esteem needs.

Such an intense preoccupation cannot last at this level and leads inevitably to a more realistic appraisal of the partner within marriage. Sometimes it brings about a strange reversal, as is seen in this anomaly of pre- and postmarital relationships: Before marriage the focus is on a loved one's good points, ignoring less desirable characteristics. After marriage the focus is on a spouse's less desirable characteristics, ignoring good points. The experiences of dating and marrying may help with esteem needs; but as the marriage proceeds and the couple settles down to the realities of family life, esteem needs may reemerge.

An alert wife realizes her husband's needs in this area. Caught up in a competitive world, a husband frequently needs something to build his shattered self-image when he returns home. In my public speaking career I frequently discover this need. Every speaker "bombs out" occasionally. When it happens to me, it is always a great joy to have a wife who is a morale builder. After such an experience, as I verbalize my conviction that I shall never be invited to make another speech, my wife replies, "Honey, even at your worst you are better than most of them." My sagging morale is given a hefty lift as she satisfies my esteem needs.

It may be that wives have a greater need for fulfillment of esteem needs than their husbands. Many a wife's life all too easily becomes circumscribed by the walls of her home. Housekeeping can be one of the most unrewarding of all activities, especially as an industrious wife sees a whole day's work undone in half an hour by a careless husband or children. When she mentions her weariness from her day's work, she may be met with, "How would you like it if you *really* had to work?" Some wives are reduced almost to begging for a small offering toward their esteem needs, "How is the meal?" "Did you notice the way I rearranged the living room?" Such a plea is sometimes completely ignored by husband and family as they rush off, leaving her with a pile of dirty dishes.

For me, church life was never a vehicle for self-expression. I grew up in the Plymouth Brethren, where we emphasized, "Let your women keep silent in your churches." So a woman never spoke or even prayed in a church gathering if men were present. When we had prayer meeting, the women met in a separate room or did not pray audibly. Decision-making conferences were all-male. Of course, women missionaries traveled across the seas and I organized a club for boys; but although women might work in the enterprise, it was completely male oriented.

After I married John and went to his church, I was pushed into the leadership of the women's missionary organization. A group of the younger women propelled me into the position; they felt it should be occupied by the minister's wife. The elderly incumbent agreed but became a thorn in my side, forever correcting everything I said or did.

NEEDS IN HUSBAND-WIFE RELATIONS

Needs	Example	Husband and Wife Activities
Physiological needs	Satisfying hunger, thirst, and sex needs	Provide shelter Prepare good meals Provide adequate sexual relations
Safety needs	Desire to live in an orderly world	Avoid intense arguments Avoid physical violence Do not threaten to leave Give a sense of security
Love needs	Sense of being loved	Loving gestures made to each other Love is verbalized, "I love you" Attitudes indicate a sense of belonging Physical contact between members of the family
Esteem needs	Having a sense of importance	Do not downgrade each other Do not make unflattering comparisons Regularly commend each other, especially in the presence of others Do not take each other for granted
Self-actualization needs	Achieving one's potentialities	Provide opportunities to realize capacities Encourage each other in actualizing potentialities

When we left that church, I resolved never to attempt a public ministry again and across the years stayed quietly in the background of my husband's ministry. He always had a heavy speaking schedule and I was happy to remain home with the boys, trying to be a good Christian mother.

Then I became aware of some vague stirring within. John had always said I was his great inspiration, and I had watched him move to prominence in his field. I gently nudged him toward a ministry in home and family life. As my family responsibilities diminished, he urged me to join his family life ministry.

It all commenced with therapy groups as he enlisted me to work as a group leader. We also developed a distinctive method of Bible study called experiential Bible study, utilizing group dynamics techniques. Then came a platform ministry. My husband was my Henry Higgins and I was his Eliza Doolittle. I discovered all sorts of talents and was soon doing readings and skits and making speeches. I think I know something of those needs for self-actualization and the wonderful way they can be satisfied in a worthwhile Christian ministry.

A century ago a young woman of the Church of England wrote to Arthur Stanley, the Dean of Westminster, "I would have given her [the church] my head, my hand, my heart. She would not have them. She told me to go back and do crochet in my mother's drawing room."[9] Fortunately for posterity, this woman, Florence Nightingale, refused to go back and do crochet. She became one of the outstanding women of the ages. She seemingly accomplished what she did not only against the blundering officialdom of her day but also against the wishes of her church. I hope we will one day learn to let women fulfill more of their needs within the church.

On one wall of my office there hangs the evidence of an interest in a rather unusual pastime—brass rubbing. I rubbed the beautiful brass engravings on four thirteenth-century tombs in Stoke Poges Church in Buckinghamshire, England. Although the rubbing process is relatively simple, it gave me a peculiar satisfaction to be able to reproduce a work of art that attracts the attention of visitors who come to see me. In one sense brass rubbing is a fulfillment of at least one of my needs for self-actualization.

The brass rubbing procedure consists of brushing the dust from the brass engraving, fastening thick black paper over the brass, securing it with masking tape, and rubbing with a special wax. As the wax is rubbed, the brass gradually emerges on the paper, rather like the potentialities that lie dormant in many people, just awaiting the right set of circumstances to call them forth.

The graveyard attached to the Stoke Poges Church where I did my rubbing was the inspiration for Thomas Gray's immortal *Elegy Written in a Country Churchyard.* The Duke of Wellington said he would rather have written that poem than won the battle of Waterloo. In his poem, Gray speculates about all the people who lie buried in the graves and says, "Some mute inglorious Milton here may rest." Some village laborer may have lived a short brutish life, never realizing his potential for taking the English language and crafting an epic from it.

Every person has some particular potential—an ability, a gift, a skill that lies like a seed in the earth awaiting the climate that will allow it to shoot, grow, and blossom. Women must be exceedingly versatile to adapt to the cycles of life and be able to make adjustments that will permit them to reach their potential. If they do not reach it, there will always be a vague dissatisfaction. Self-actualization means individuals must have a sense of attaining their potential. As Maslow said, "A musician must make music, an artist must paint, a poet must write if he is to be ultimately happy."[10] The family should be the primary unit that provides the environment within which individuals can meet their needs and move on to become self-actualizing persons.

CHAPTER 3

Farewell Master, Welcome Partner

 onscious of the importance of a positive attitude in her relationships
with her husband, she is resolved always to be a help rather than
a hindrance to him.

Prov. 31:12

GIMEL

In 1539, Henry VIII of England, avaricious, obese, sensual,
and a three-time loser in the game of matrimony, paused to contem-
plate his poor track record in the marriage stakes. His marriage to
Catherine of Aragon ended in divorce; he had sent Anne Boleyn to the
chopping block; and Jane Seymour, who had given him a son, had died
shortly after the birth. Looking around for a new queen, Henry was
caught between his amorous desires and political necessity. The politi-
cally expedient course of action was to marry Anne, daughter of the
Protestant German Duke of Cleves. But Henry, who had an eye for the
ladies, wanted to be sure Anne came up to his expectations of feminine
attractiveness before pressing the matter. He therefore sent a mission
to Cleves that included Hans Holbein, the court painter, telling the
artist, "I put more trust in your brush than in the reports of my
courtiers."

Working in Cleves on Anne's portrait, Holbein found himself torn
between painting an honest portrait and succumbing to the pressures
of Henry's courtiers. Before Holbein left England, Sir Thomas Crom-

well, the king's trusted adviser, had warned him to bring back a *beautiful* portrait of Anne. But Anne was a large-boned, bovine woman with a pocked face, unsophisticated and dull witted. If he painted her as she was, Holbein could offend the woman who might be the next queen of England and certainly frustrate the plans of Thomas Cromwell and his political cronies. Expediency won out as Holbein used his remarkable painting ability to produce a magnificent portrait of Anne, her insipid features framed in velvet, beautiful jewels, and brocades. Her pock-marked skin appeared flawless. His powerful composition enhanced Anne's better features and omitted most of her defects.

One look at the painting convinced Henry he was about to wed a continental beauty and he enthusiastically signed the marriage contract. When at last he met Anne, Henry was outraged and ordered Cromwell to find a remedy. But the contracts had been signed and the king was compelled to go through with the marriage. Six months later, Henry had the marriage declared null and void and proceeded to arrest Sir Thomas Cromwell, sending him to his death in the Tower of London.

The portrait of Anne of Cleves has been described as an exquisite work of art but also as the woman who never was. It was simply the product of Holbein's imagination and typical of how men are prone to make women as they would like them to be. This is most clearly seen in relationships between husbands and wives. Across the years women have been relegated to an inferior position within the marriage relationship; and, unfortunately, the Bible has all too frequently been misinterpreted and used as a means of reinforcing this inferior role.

Note that I say "misinterpreted." Look at Proverbs 31:10–31, a portrayal of the relationship of husband and wife as two interacting personalities. The husband has an important position in the community and the wife is engaged in a multiplicity of activities. From the detailed treatment of her many enterprises, it would be easy to conclude she was the better of the two. Her husband does not dominate her; and despite all her activities, she is aware of his work and will do nothing to hinder him. This discussion ushers us into a consideration of a husband and wife and the new math of marriage. The mathematics of marriage has passed through three distinctive phases: $1+1=1$, $1+1=2$, $1+1=3$.

A NOBLE IDEA AND ITS DISTORTIONS

The formula $1+1=1$ is the oldest of all and stems from Genesis 2:23–24. When a delighted Adam looked upon his new bride, he said, "This is now bone of my bone and flesh of my flesh, she shall be called woman because she was taken out of man. Therefore shall a man leave his father and mother and cleave unto his wife and they shall be one flesh." Following this concept, one man plus one woman equals one flesh. The statement is obviously true in the physical sense, and many societies do not look upon any marriage as valid unless it has been consummated.

A number of valid ideas flow from the one-flesh assumption. One is that marriage is permanent. The biblical idea of marriage is a commitment of two people to each other in a lifelong relationship, and this is inherent in the idea of one flesh. As C. S. Lewis has said, a surgeon would need some compelling reason to cut a living body in halves. The dismemberment of a marriage relationship is a concession to the frailty of human beings and represents a falling short of the ideal. "What God hath joined together let not man put asunder."

A second valid idea from the one-flesh assumption is the order of loyalties in marriage. Born into the context of a family, the child grows into adulthood and then in marriage moves into a new commitment. "For this cause shall a man leave his father and mother" (Mark 10:7). If this statement were taken literally, it would mean an end to in-law problems.

A third idea is the highest form of self-love. In the epistle of the Ephesians, Paul takes up this idea of one flesh and gives it an interesting twist. His argument is that if two people in marriage become "one flesh," when a man loves his wife, he loves himself. This is the best type of self-love.

The distortion of this $1+1=1$ idea takes several forms. One misinterpretation has been the concept of a symbiotic relationship within which neither husband nor wife can function without the other, as seen in the case of Judy and Greg Dickinson.

An attractive twenty-year-old, Judy had a strong streak of altruism and moved very naturally into social service activities. Majoring in working with the deaf in college, she met a good-looking, partially deaf man named Greg Meritt. His hearing problem had left him with some speech difficulties, causing him to be rather diffident about entering into conversation. Immediately attracted to each other, they soon established a relationship in which she became his means of communication with others. She used sign language to pass on any message she felt he might have missed, and he signed to her and she spoke any statement he wished to make. Their romance developed rapidly and they married. When Greg decided on graduate school, he faced a crisis because Judy had not yet completed college and would be unable to do so at the school where he was to study. So she put aside her college career and accompanied him to all his classes. He seldom spoke, signing to Judy and letting her verbalize the response. So developed a strong symbiotic relationship in which all communication with Greg had to go through Judy.

This might be called a true $1+1=1$ relationship, but it was an awful waste of abilities in so many ways. Greg needed to speak and develop his expressive communication skills. Judy should have been getting her education. The time she spent unnecessarily interpreting for him could have been used to complete her own college degree. Judy had no life at all apart from Greg.

Possibly the worst distortion of $1+1=1$ is that this implies a hierarchy within the marriage relationship. Although God stands at the highest level, the husband, as head of the family, is next and after him the wife, with the children coming next. In this chain of command concept the wife not only stands as number two but must be willing at any time to have her views vetoed by the all-knowing husband.

Consider this scenario. Jill and Howard Masters have what they consider a good marriage and are trying to live by Christian principles. Howard is of average intelligence. He managed to plod through college and sighed with relief when his degree was conferred. Jill was an exceptionally good student whose professors predicted would pursue a Ph.D. Jill and Howard met at the campus Christian group. She was attracted by Howard's fine Christian character; she had always wanted a Christian marriage, so she found it easy to love him despite his less than exceptional intellectual abilities. Jill's father took Howard into the family business, where he was reliable rather than brilliant.

One evening Howard approached the question of a lake house. A client had told him about a house at the lake that was a steal at $60,000. He pointed out how wonderful it would be for them to go each weekend to the lake house. Of course, they could come home for Sunday school. They would be able to have friends out with them. What should Jill do? Should she sit down and show Howard that they can barely make payments on their existing car and house? The lake house would put them under a crushing burden of debt. They are both active in church on Sundays and would have little time to spend at the lake. Should she then conclude with, "Howard I'm sorry I can't go along with you on this"? Or should Jill explain all of the above and when Howard says he still wants the lake house no matter what, respond, "Thank God for the lake house. Let's make a down payment"?

The second answer is correct if you believe in the chain of command. A woman is a mindless creation who has no ability to challenge her omnipotent husband's decisions. The concept of $1+1=1$ is a noble biblical idea, but these distortions have turned off many intelligent women and caused them to look in other directions.

A DOUBTFUL DIVISION

With the advent of the feminist movement and the turbulent era of the 1960s, women began to demand their rights. No longer content to live in terms of their husband's ambitions and aspirations, women felt they had a right to "do their own thing." Marriage was a relationship of two equals. Husband is husband and wife is wife and never the twain shall meet. Living together for the convenience of housekeeping, maybe rearing of children, and convenient sexual congress, they both have their separate existence. Separate bank accounts may ensure financial independence and a strong-minded woman will retain her maiden name.

Part of this movement was the increasing use of contracts. One report on Jacqueline Kennedy's marriage to Aristotle Onassis stated they had drawn up a 170-point contract that covered every possible detail of life, with particular emphasis on the individual rights of both parties to the agreement. The following are examples of points often covered in a marriage contract:

1. The wife's right to use her maiden name or any other name she chooses.
2. What surname the children will have: husband's, wife's, a hyphenated combination, a neutral name, or the name the children choose when they reach a certain age.
3. Birth control: whether or not, what kind, and who uses it. (One couple—the wife cannot use the pill—splits the responsibility fifty-fifty. Half the time she uses a diaphragm; the other half he uses a condom.)
4. Whether to have children, to adopt them, and if so how many.
5. How the children will be brought up.
6. Where the couple will live. (Will the husband be willing to move if the wife gets a job offer she wants to take? Separate bedrooms? Separate apartments?)
7. How child care and housework will be divided. (The spouse who earns less should not be penalized for the inequities of the economic world by having to do a larger share.)
8. Financial arrangement. (If husband and wife are both wage earners, there are three basic possibilities: [1] They pool their income, pay expenses, and divide any surplus. [2] They pay shares of expenses proportional to their incomes. Each keeps whatever he or she has left. [3] They each pay half the expenses. Each keeps what he or she has left.)
9. Sexual rights and freedoms. (Although any arrangement other than monogamy would clearly be against public policy, in practice some people make arrangements such as having Tuesdays off from one another.)
10. Husband's consent to abortion in advance.

There is certainly much to be said for contracts in marriage in that they help the parties have a clearer understanding of their expectations. This is particularly true with regard to premarital conflicts. Employing this rational approach would help eliminate the "love will find a way" idea. However, problems arise with the contract. Marriage itself is a contract, but documents covering such points as listed seem opposed to the Christian idea of marriage. Considering what marriage has meant and that it was intended to be the $1+1=2$ concept evokes Dr. Johnson's comment concerning women preachers, "It's like a dog walking on its hind legs. It isn't done well and one wonders why it is done at all."[11]

I was raised in a home with the $1+1=1$ concept and its implication of a hierarchical system. My mother was a devout believer in the Bible and accepted the idea that the husband was the head of the wife, women should not speak in church, and as a symbol of their subservient position should keep their heads covered while attending meetings. I never saw my mother go to any meeting without her hat. One of our dear friends who belonged to the same group would carry this to its logical conclusion and when someone prayed, as they often did, in her home, she would immediately cover her head with some convenient handkerchief or piece of material. All of this signaled her acknowledgment of the subservient position of a wife to her husband.

The major problem was that my mother was the spiritual giant of our family. My father was a quiet man. A hard worker, my father's work on ships kept him periodically away from home. He had probably learned to live a quiet, secluded life by spending so much time at sea. To while away the hours on the ship, he learned to play the "Jews harp" and would sometimes sit in a room quietly playing. After returning from a sea trip, following a good meal, he would go down to the nearby river to work on his small boat. Rather shy and reserved, he was awkward in company.

My mother was in complete and full control and she certainly knew how to manage her home. In many ways she had enlightened ideas that were ahead of her time. In a day when family planning was not done by evangelical Christians, she would warn her daughters about the burdens of childbearing and exhort them to plan their families well.

Mother was a beautiful illustration of the way Christian women would give assent to the proposition that the husband was the head and director of the family, then proceed subtly to manipulate the situation to have their way. I often think this "double standard" gets pretty close to being dishonest. I remember one of the most dominant women I ever knew confessing to me how difficult she found it to maintain a truly Christian attitude of submission then heroically declaring she had nevertheless managed to obtain this "with the Lord's help." Having seen how she ruled her family with an iron hand, I restrained the impulse to say "poppycock."

My husband and I are partners. For years I followed the chain of command idea that John was the head of the house. I sometimes joked, "My husband is the head of our house; I'm just the neck." At the beginning of our marriage John wrote all the checks. He was busy with his work and did not particularly like the details of such activity as reconciling the checkbook, so I gradually moved into the role of family treasurer and enjoyed it. For many years now I have made most of the decisions about how the money is going to be spent. It was an excellent preparation for a small business I later became involved in.

When I was working on the checks one day, John asked, "Why do you sign your name Mrs. John Drakeford? Don't you have a name of your own?" We had many discussions about this. I always imagined only widowed or divorced women would sign Mrs. Robina Drakeford, however I noticed some liberated women were keeping their own surnames even though married. I was not ready for this, but just coming to the idea of writing Mrs. Robina Drakeford gave me a sense of individual status apart from my husband.

As the partnership idea took hold, we carried it over into our work. John began to insist he not go on a family life conference without me, so we became partners in our work. One strange situation came when I was invited to speak at a meeting in a distant city. John urged me to go but teased me that whereas he would not go without me, I was willing to go without him.

I have always been fascinated by the biblical characters Priscilla and Acquilla. These two worked side by side as tentmakers to earn their living. They are mentioned five times in the New Testament, and on two of these occasions Priscilla is mentioned before her husband, Acquilla. Considering the importance attached to the order of names in

the Bible, it becomes clear they were partners, with no idea of a
dominant husband and a subservient wife.

A HEALTHY PARTNERSHIP

The new notion that appears to be emerging, which is compatible
with the portrayal of the ideal woman in Proverbs 31, is that two people
in marriage are partners. This biblical ideal wife has a wide variety of
interest in agriculture, weaving, real estate, household management,
and making and wearing clothes. The husband, being a political leader,
spends much of his time at his politics, in which he enjoys a widespread
reputation. "Her husband is known in the gates where he sitteth
amongst the elders of the land" (Prov. 31:23); so each of them has
individual and satisfying personal interests.

But this husband and wife also have areas of shared interest. Like
some recurring refrain in a musical masterpiece, in the midst of this
paean the ideal woman's husband is mentioned directly or by implication five times. She is said to be his most precious possession: "If you
can find a truly good wife, she is worth more than precious gems"
(Prov. 31:10). She interacts with him by supplying his needs and giving
him grounds for trusting her: "Her husband can trust her, and she will
richly satisfy his needs" (Prov. 31:11). She efficiently cares for and
establishes a good relationship with their children: "Her children stand
up and bless her" (Prov. 31:28). Then he realizes what her needs are
and gives her his unstinted praise: "There are many fine women in the
world but you are the best of them all" (Prov. 31:29).

John Wesley, the founder of Methodism, was uncertain about marriage because he felt a wife might be a hindrance to his work in
preaching the Gospel. As his ministry went on, he began to see how
a woman could help and referred to Grace Murray as "my right arm."
When at last he did take the matrimonial plunge, he did it precipitous-
ly. He married a widow named Molly Vazielle after knowing her just
a few weeks. The marriage was a disaster. Molly, apparently paranoid,
became a constant source of embarrassment, annoyance, and frustration. She spied on him, read his letters, and destroyed valuable materials. The situation continued to deteriorate until they finally separated.

Wesley later wrote in uncharacteristic bitterness, "If you were to live for a thousand years you could not undo the mischief you have done.... I bid you farewell."[1]

What a tragic example of the way two people can hurt each other in marriage and a tremendous contrast with our ideal wife, of whom it was written concerning her relationships with her husband, "She will not hinder him but help him all her life" (Prov. 31:12).

CHAPTER 4

Hands Busy at the Pleasures of Her Heart

oing something for the pure joy of it, she searches for and busily spins wool and flax.

Prov. 31:13

DALETH

Superwoman is human! She needs some time away from her busy routine responsibilities, so she engages in some activities just because she likes them. She has a hobby of searching out a particular type of wool and flax and spins these textiles into products she can proudly display to her friends and neighbors. One version emphasizes the joy she experiences in doing something she likes and translates this verse, "Her hands are busy at the pleasure of her heart."

A highly respected and successful woman executive, retired and living on a nice retirement income, apparently had it made, being able to do whatever she wished. When a journalist asked her what she would do differently if she could start again, she said she would learn to play. Every woman needs something she does for the pleasure of her heart, a hobby, something she does in her leisure time that takes her mind off her responsibilities and lets her relax. All work and no play makes Jill a dull girl. Just look at the paths a hobby led Robina into.

When his doctor told John cycling would strengthen the muscles of his leg and help a troublesome knee, he little knew what an interest he was creating in that eager-beaver husband of mine. It was not long before John was absorbed in all aspects of cycling: subscribing to magazines, borrowing books from the library, visiting with groups of cyclists, and haunting cycling shops. I have always been an exercise nut. I play tennis and swim; but they have a disadvantage in that they require a special setting and arranging of schedules, which is time consuming and often inconvenient. Here was an exercise activity that required little more than wheeling the cycle out of the garage and pedaling off down the street. Happy associations came to mind. When we were first married, the church we pastored provided transportation for my husband in the form of a church bicycle and a generous family gave me a bicycle so I could ride around with him as we did our pastoral calling. In a short time we were mounting our bikes and spending a good proportion of the day riding around the community in our pastoral work or down to the beach for our daily surfing.

It was like history repeating itself as we bought a pair of bikes and began a new hobby. I very naturally turned to browsing through the literature my husband had accumulated. I discovered it opened the door to a wonderful world of nostalgia. Naturally, I recollected the song about love and marriage that has stood the test of time.

> Daisy Daisy give me your answer do
> I'm half crazy all for the love of you
> It won't be a stylish marriage,
> I can't afford a carriage
> But you'll look sweet
> Upon the seat of a bicycle built for two.

Written by Harry Dacre, this song took the world by storm and is still sung with great enthusiasm at gay nineties banquets and other nostalgia events. It conjures up images of men and women, straw hatted, handlebar mustachioed man, high-necked and pleated-bloused woman, sweeping along on their tandem bicycle.

That clothing opened up a fascinating field of study for a woman interested in clothes. One fashion authority claimed the bicycle may have been the most important single factor in the emancipation of women from the all-enclosing, body-squeezing garments of the Victorian era. As they mounted their bicycles, women moved from dresses to knickerbockers, stockings, and high boots; a simple shirt with collar and tie; and later divided skirts. Girls' ankles were daringly revealed. Scandalized males did their best to halt the brazen practices of the fairer sex, even going so far as to introduce laws into Congress forbidding the wearing of such apparel by women. Women still wear an article of clothing, albeit very modest by present-day standards, that recalls the effect of the bicycle on feminine clothes: "pedal pushers."

I found some historical bypaths. The golden age of cycling came in the so-called "gay nineties," when cycling was more than a means of transportation or even a sport. It was a craze. In this era, every town had its bicycling club and the place to be was the cycle races. The craze affected male-female relationships; and the humble bicycle became the vehicle of love for quite a number of years. A romance often began with an invitation to go cycling and gradually grew as a young man invited the lady of his choice to join him on a bicycle built for two. This new mobility for young people gave rise to apprehensions on the part of parents and others concerned about the morals of the rising generation. Preachers uttered dark warnings of the dangers of the new mobility, with its potentialities for hanky-panky.

Then there was that fascinating use of a bicycle in romance as a gift to a beloved. "Diamond Jim" Brady outdid fellow suitors with their bouquets of flowers when he presented actress Lillian Russell with a gold-plated bicycle complete with mother-of-pearl handlebars and spokes encrusted with chips of diamonds, emeralds, rubies, and sapphires. The bicycle was then valued at ten thousand dollars; and Miss Russell took it on tour, suitably packed in a blue, plush-lined morocco case.

With my newly awakened interest, I was somewhat disappointed to discover a more sophisticated generation is not too impressed with cycling and looks back to yesteryear with a chuckle, as illustrated by a second verse to Daisy Bell.

> Michael, Michael, here is my answer dear,
> I can't cycle it makes me feel so queer,
> If you can't afford a carriage,

> Call off the blooming marriage,
> For I'll be blowed if I'll be towed,
> On a bicycle built for two.

Moreover, the bicycle that brought so many new freedoms to women is now viewed with suspicion by some of the new generation. One authority on cycling notes that women's liberation has just about put male-female tandems out of business. He claims that women cyclists express their disdain for the tandem by saying they are not about to take a back seat to any man, particularly on a bike.

The bicycle seldom qualifies for serious consideration as a means of transportation today, even though many, myself included, wish it would. But it is a hobby, something done just for the joy of it all. I have discovered a satisfying hobby may build better relationships between a husband and wife. Of course, there are occasions in some hobbies where it may not benefit the process, as when a husband insists on pointing out his wife's shortcomings in her tennis serve. However, it has some interesting possibilities, as may be seen in tandem cycling.

After a period of cycling on individual bicycles and inspired by "Daisy Bell" John and I decided to invest in a tandem bike. Although we were by now seasoned cyclists, we soon discovered that riding tandem was different from riding individual bikes. Even mounting the machines requires a different technique. I rode on the rear (in cycling jargon, the "stoker" as opposed to the "captain," caring for steering at the front) and soon found that if I mounted first, there was a good chance John would give me a kick in the solar plexus as he swung his leg over the bike frame. So we planned it carefully and agreed on the order in which mounting was to take place. Similarly, in dismounting I had to be off first.

Once underway, John had a good clear view of the pathway ahead and so became the lookout, ready to warn of troubles that lay in wait. In short order we developed a whole group of new words to use in communicating with each other. Such words included "bump" when a ridge appeared in the road, "lift" when one of those bone-shattering chuck holes loomed ahead, "down" when necessary to reduce speed, and "ease up" when one partner was pushing too hard. Negotiating a

CONSIDERATIONS IN SELECTING A HOBBY

Temperament. What would you enjoy doing? Do not select something that is going to be a burden. Choose a field that is not too difficult, in line with your interests and unusual enough to attract some attention.

Space and location. If you live in a small apartment, it would not be wise to collect bulky objects that have to be stored. Woodworking will not be appropriate unless you have some place, such as a garage, where you can work. There are many wonderful hobbies that can be carried on in a small space. Select accordingly.

Finances. Some hobbies can run into a lot of money. Check out the cost before you start.

Action. There is no sense in always thinking you would like to do it. Try the following plan:

1. Take a good overall view of your hobby. Visit around, look in the shops that carry the materials, discuss it with your friends, and read books about it.

2. Investigate the fellowship involved. Is there a club or some group of people interested? Some groups have regular meetings with lectures, demonstrations, and so forth.

3. Subscribe to a magazine in the field. You will find helpful articles that will bring new aspects and enrich your hobby. Sometimes the advertisements alone are worth the money.

4. Go about it in orderly steps. Do not outlay a great deal of money at first. Try the simple things; then move into the more complex.

One problem. One woman I know became so interested in and competent at her hobby that she went into business and made a nice living at it. The difficulty was that it no longer was something she did for fun and recreation—she had to find another hobby.

corner called for special teamwork. Although my husband controlled the front wheel, bikes are turned by leaning to the right or left. If I decided to turn, I could do it; but it would be a disaster. Similarly, I gave all the hand signals while John concentrated on keeping us on course. When we really learned to work together and keep the channels of communication wide open, we went spinning along.

But our conversation was not limited to the mechanics of cycling. We discussed houses, lawns, trees, friendly and hostile dogs, and things having to do with our family. Then we met other cyclists and various other hardy souls who braved the 6 A.M. darkness to get some exercise. Add to this the feeling of well-being when after an hour of cycling we showered, sat down to breakfast, and opened our Bibles and hearts to talk with Almighty God.

As a footnote, I might add we ride with a gentleman friend who is quite an athlete and a real pacesetter. When we mounted our tandem, we discovered tandem riders are the hotrodders of the cycling world and two can generally travel at least 10 percent faster than one. It gave us a great feeling of satisfaction as we drew away from our athletic friend and reinforced the idea that "two are better than one"—a pretty good concept for a husband and wife.

The woman with a hobby who worked at "the pleasures of her heart" found some wonderful satisfactions in life. Every woman needs a hobby. If you are interested in getting started, the information in the box below may help you.

CHAPTER 5

A Family Marches on Its Stomach

 ver seeking to provide a varied diet for her family, she purchases a variety of foods shipped in by importers.

Prov. 31:14

HEH

Concerned about the health of her family, superwife made sure their diet was not only wholesome and nutritious but varied and appetizing. Early in the morning, before the food was picked over, she hastened down to the marketplace to examine the goods being sold there by importers. In this day of Solomon's grandeur, ships of Tarshish regularly sailed westward, returning to the port of Joppa laden with products from Mediterranean lands. On the eastern shores, Phoenician sailors navigated their vessels to and from the port of Elath on the Red Sea to Arabia, Africa, and as far as India. Pushing her way through the jostling crowds, superwife purchases rare fruits, vegetables, fish, poultry, and meat for her family. This food shopping activity caused the writer to say, "She is like the merchant's ships, she brings her food from afar" (Prov. 31:14, KJV).

I guess you could say I am a child of the sea. I was born in Troon, Scotland, home of the famous golf course. Our little town was equally well known as a seaside resort looking out over the Irish Sea. The sea and ships were a way of life for us. Many of the ships built in the Firth of Clyde came sailing down from those famous shipyards, and we lined up along the beach to watch the monarchs of the sea proudly taking their trial runs before being turned over to their new owners. My father captained his own small vessel, the Pride of Morne, *in which he and his brother labored diligently transporting goods around the coastal ports of the United Kingdom and across the sea to Ireland.*

But that same sea that throughout the years had provided our living with a strange perversity suddenly snatched our financial resources from us. Sitting deep in the water with a heavy cargo of potatoes, the Pride of Morne *was overtaken by a storm at sea and driven onto the rocks. Both ship and cargo were lost, bringing financial devastation to our family.*

My father went to work for others in the shipping business. One monumental project was to sail a newly constructed ship from the nearby Firth of Clyde to its owners in far-off Australia. After a dreary three-month trip, the ship steamed into Port Jackson and my father gazed upon the beautiful Sydney Harbour and contrasted the sparkling sunny water and golden sand beaches with the cold water and leaden skies of Scotland. He knew immediately he had found the one place he wanted to live. So he obtained a position with a coastal shipping line and wrote back to Scotland to tell my mother to sell all our possessions, gather our family together, pack, take the trip to London, and set out on the long voyage to Australia.

I grew up in Australia, where we lived on the seacoast, and there I met and married John. Years later we moved to the United States. My husband had flown over previously; and my sons and I booked passages on the British ship Orsova, *making its maiden voyage across the Pacific. For three weeks we luxuriated in shipboard living. Climbing down the gangway in San Francisco, we left the way of the sea to take up residence in landlocked Fort Worth, Texas. When I read of this woman that she is "like the merchant's ships," I feel much akin with her.*

The U.S. Bicentennial in 1976 brought with it many unusual events, none of which was more spectacular than the parade of tall ships. From all over the world nations sent sailing ships that sailed into New York Harbor and provided a never to be forgotten sight as they moved along in an impressive procession. Such an assemblage of sailing ships will probably never be seen again for the very good reason that the sailing ship is now an expensive luxury rather than an economical means of transportation. In Solomon's day, sailing tied the ancient world together and brought the goods of many lands to the Jerusalem marketplace.

The ideal wife worked at making attractive meals for her family. Customarily, the Hebrews of that day had a morning morsel and then the two major meals at noon and in the evening when the sun had set. How she relished that meal hour as her family gathered around the bountiful board. She surely would be surprised if she dropped into a modern home, where the family meal with all the household gathered around is rapidly disappearing.

Cooking itself used to be a fine art. Until just a few years ago, a woman came into marriage skilled in the art of preparing meals. She had served an apprenticeship with her mother, who supervised her efforts. As they worked together, mother passed on some of her prized recipes to her daughter, in contrast to her response to a visitor who sought the same recipe only to find it a closely guarded secret. Thus the cooking art had an air of mystery about it. A woman famous for her apple strudel would confide in her daughter that it took a pinch of this and a handful of that, no more. That art has almost gone. Ask for a recipe and the hostess will openly admit she got it from *Good Housekeeping Cookbook* on page 37, where all the ingredients are listed in very precise, measureable quantities. Or, worse still, the hostess admits it is a mix and that using this prepared mix she can produce an angel food cake that rises higher than any she could make from scratch.

In superwife's day, preparing a meal was quite a chore as she went about grinding the wheat and barley, preparing the fruit dressing, and cooking the poultry or meat. Her modern sister has learned an easier way and been introduced to the advantages of frozen sandwiches, TV dinners, instant breakfast food, and packaged snacks. Unfortunately, all this has further divided families. One building contractor recently reported that contrary to the normal expectation that a business would avoid competition, fast food chains are anxious to locate in close prox-

imity to each other. If the family should have a modicum of unity and
drive up in one car, they could immediately "split," each family member to his own taco, corndog, or hamburger. The sitdown meal with
the family gathered around is rapidly becoming a memory.

*Using group techniques with people, we sometimes ask the partici-
pants to answer a number of questions about their early life so they can
have an opportunity to express themselves about their childhood. One
of the questions, is "What was the warmest room in your home?" Most
people answer it was the kitchen, the place where the meals were
prepared and eaten and the family gathered together to discuss the
affairs of the day. I remember reading about a study of communal
enterprises by Rosabeth Kanter. Her study showed that every one of
the successful groups had regular group meetings.*[1] *But where are the
regular meetings of the family today?*

*The family meal is the ideal vehicle for group interaction and food
is the great enhancer of communication. Today, however, families do
not gather around the table as a group for a meal. They drift in one
or two at a time, grab a snack, and go on their way. One study showed
that if a family sat together for a meal three times a week, they did well.
When they did eat, it was not the cohesive, spirited gathering of
yesteryear, a situation brought about in part because two out of every
three families watch television during mealtime. Eating has become a
highly individual experience.*

Here are some guidelines for a good mealtime experience:

1. *All the members of the family should assemble and begin the
   meal at the same time.*
2. *Family rituals are important. Why not hold hands and have a
   family member ask the blessing? On other occasions you could
   repeat it together.*
3. *Share the table-waiting duties. Do not let mother be the unpaid
   waitress.*
4. *Turn off the television. It is impossible to carry on an intelligent
   conversation while the television demands both your ears and
   your eyes.*
5. *Try to involve all the family in conversation. Invite them to report*

on their day, the good things and the bad things. Ask them if anyone has heard a joke or a funny story and hear them out.

6. *Make your mealtime a celebration. Remember the birthdays of family members. What about religious and patriotic holidays? This would be a good time to celebrate them.*

7. *Have you considered a family altar? Why not try a time of Bible reading and praying?*

8. *Try to cultivate the practice of all the family remaining for the whole meal. Do not have them catching a bite and running.*

9. *At the completion of the meal, let all the family work at cleaning up. Pass around responsibilities. It can be fun. Remember, too, many hands make light work.*

One outstanding psychiatrist has told us that the first natural impulse is to try to feed a loved one. If eating occupies such an important part in the development of love life, it will naturally follow that mealtime experiences will have special significance not only during courting days but right through family life. From this chapter's verse in Proverbs, we can see superwife may be setting an example that many a modern family might well emulate by making more out of the family meal.

CHAPTER 6

Beating the Housecoat Syndrome

 eeling concerned about her family, she rises early to prepare breakfast and plan the day's activities.

Prov. 31:15

VAV

President Carter was addressing the assembled group of workers from the Department of Health, Education and Welfare. As part
of his introductory remarks, he noted this department had the responsibility for unemployed people and said, "A couple of months ago I was
unemployed myself. I now have a job and it pays pretty well." His
audience roared with laughter, as did the Jacobsen family, gathered
around the TV set, watching the event on the evening news.

Mrs. Jacobsen, who had passed the family on her way to the table
with a portion of the evening meal, paused for a moment to catch the
president's remarks but did not join in the laughter. Instead she said,
sarcastically, "I'm sure glad that he's satisfied with his job and its pay.
And thank his lucky stars he's not a housewife with a family who
doesn't ever notice all the work she does."

The note in his wife's voice caused Jim Jacobsen to comment,
"Watch it honey. You might get fired. You ought to be thankful you
have got such a good job." "Good job! It's the only job I know that
has no set hours, is completely unappreciated, has no future. If I work
hard picking up after this untidy bunch, I wear myself out and you kids

never learn how to keep your rooms. And one day you will all be gone and I will have spent my years developing and cultivating a skill of absolutely no value to me."

HOUSEWIVES' COMPLAINTS

The way things are going, it may not be long before a new group of demonstrators join civil righters, gay liberationists, and other dissidents in demanding their rights. Women carrying babies, wearing aprons, and wielding kitchen utensils may be carrying signs saying "Slaves of the house unite" and singing "We Shall Overcome." A new restiveness has come over the people who for so long have been the epitome of patience and self-sacrifice as they enter upon what has been called the revolt of the American housewife. The list of complaints makes impressive reading.

One complaint is the lack of distinction between working hours and time off. A housewife looks after her husband, who starts at nine and quits at five with three weeks vacation each year, and contrasts the long hours she has to work. One study showed many wives are working fifty-five hours plus per week on a seven-day-week job. When vacation times rolls around, it may mean a change of scenery but all the regular responsibilities. If a husband is sick, he can take time off from work and expects to get some special attention; but if a wife feels ill she can just forget it. There are some husbands who get completely frustrated if their wife is ill and they are pushed into household responsibilities. One wife expressed it, "Although he demands and gets special attention when he is sick, my husband believes I have no right to ever be ill."

The situation may have some religious implications and superwife of Old Testament times must have been aware of these. For the Jew, the Ten Commandments, the Decalog, were of the utmost importance because they told of ten great principles of living. The commandment about keeping the Sabbath day is the longest of them all; it spells out the importance of resting from all work on at least one day of the week. Members of the household who should rest are named, "On that day you are to do no work of any kind, nor shall your son, daughter, or

slaves—whether man or woman—or your cattle, or your house guests"
(Exod. 20:10, LB). That includes about everybody—except the
housewife. Apparently she has to work on. The servants, children,
houseguests, and even the cattle have a day off, but no rest for the wife;
her work continues.

Many a wife feels the need to flex her physical or intellectual muscles. Her husband can be off to the ballgame with the boys or take a
day or two for hunting. But when she wants to take a class at the "Y"
or a course at the community college, she may have to ask him to
babysit. He finds it difficult to see her point of view. One woman
reacted, "What's wrong with him? I don't complain when he plays
golf."

Another complaint is a sense that housework is of no great importance. If she decides really to excel at her housework, a wife may have
difficulty persuading other family members it is a worthwhile enterprise. One mother verbalized her frustration, "I spend all this time
cleaning house. It is not the most inspiring work in the world. Then
the kids come in and undo all I have done in about thirty minutes. Talk
about lack of respect for another's work." Later, when the children are
grown and she might hope for some understanding, the kids will offer
some advice, "Why don't you get a job, mother?" And mother will
have a feeling that what she does counts for little. One woman expressed it, "When my husband comes in and says, 'What did you do
all day?' I resent it. When I start to tell him all my frustrations about
the day's activity, he answers, 'How would you like it if you had to work
like me?' "

The feeling is so widespread that when a group of women formed
the Martha Movement, named for Martha, who worked while her sister
sat and listened to Jesus (Luke 10:38–42), aiming at a new status for
housewives, it rapidly spread across the country. The founder says the
movement is saying, "Hey, it's okay to be a homemaker but you should
have some status and respect for your skills." Praise, which is so sweet
to everybody's ears, seldom gets to the housewife. From those for
whom she has worked so hard, making the house immaculate and doing
everything just right, she seldom hears, "You've done a fantastic job."

Some women object to being known as a housewife. One woman

insisted she be called a homemaker, saying, "The word housewife seem to indicate I am married to my house. I am not." In a day when the business world has discovered a new title is often a greater motivator than a raise and the garbage man is a sanitation engineer and the barber is a hair stylist, it may be time to use some new terms, like domestic engineer, household executive, atmosphere creator, or home manager, to bring at least a modicum of dignity to the task.

Another complaint is that a homemaker's life may be isolated and out of the mainstream of life. Confined to the house with a couple of small children, her main activities being to care for them, shop for groceries, and keep the home clean, the homemaker does not have many opportunities for meaningful social relationships. Her husband has his work, where he is meeting other people; school age children have their peers; but a homemaker's contacts are mainly limited to discussing the matters of her home and family with other people. She sometimes feels everyone else is growing and developing but her world is standing still. She is being left behind. The only adult she ever comes in contact with may be the actors in the soap opera she watches daily, an activity that leaves her depressed by the mountains of misfortunes that befall the characters. When children later leave home, she will need social skills in relating to adults; but will she have lost them?

Homemakers frequently have a sense of being less than successful. An honors graduate from a prestigious university said, "I just cannot develop an interest in chasing dirt." Many a woman feels less than fulfilled as she faces the monotonous rounds of keeping house. One survey showed that half (57 percent) of the full-time housewives interviewed felt they are not competent at their household tasks.[1] This lack of sense of competence left many women frustrated and led them into a cycle. Feeling inadequate, they came to hate housework and became more careless about their domestic responsibilities. The more frustrated they feel, the less they are inclined to work. The result is a frustrated woman who has a sense of being trapped in a situation.

Another homemaker complaint concerns the lack of self-identity. Before she was married, June Haskell was vividly aware of her status. She remembers being introduced on one occasion to a young man who said, "Not *the* June Haskell?" It made her feel good. Now busily employed about the household, she works at motivating her husband, keeping him well dressed, and caring for the children. When a new department store opened in her neighborhood, at their invitation she applied for a credit card and discovered it was in her husband's name. Now she is Paul's wife or Suzie's mother, an identity something less than satisfying.

Homemakers are vulnerable to economic disaster. The traditional way of looking at marriage has been as a trade-off. He earns the money; she cares for the household. Frequently, he feels that because he "earns the money," he is entitled to be the treasurer, deciding how it will be spent. He may be "generous" to his wife but still make the decisions. She assumes she has the legal right to support, but it does not always turn out that way. One feminist lawyer states the case clearly, "A husband's duty to support his wife amounts to little more than what he chooses to give her."

The situation is so seriously regarded by some women that a new organization, known as the Wages for Housewives Committee, has come into existence. Its aim is to gain recognition of housework as serious labor. Consequently, everybody who does housework, regardless of sex or marital status, should be paid. A spokeswoman for the organization states their case, "If you have to cook meals for the family everyday and have very little money, the work becomes enormous. It is there day after day, year after year, and it is taken for granted. Sometimes we work as long as ninety hours a week. And there is no work schedule, no time off and no medical insurance."[2] The committee suggests adequate payment of a salary from a fund contributed to by industry and government, both of whom profit from a housewife's labor in taking care of her husband and children and raising future workers for the labor market. It would hardly be wise for a housewife to rush out and start spending her "pay," but the very fact the idea is being touted is an indication of many women's frustration at having no money of their own.

With one out of every three marriages ending in divorce, a dependent wife's life may be a chancy business. Recent figures indicate only one in seven divorcees receive alimony, fewer than 50 percent are awarded child support, a majority of husbands welch on child support, and if a marriage lasts less than twenty years, a wife's share of her husband's old age benefits will be nil. She may have short-circuited her own education to marry, even worked at putting her husband through college. Now she is ill prepared to enter the job market. A disillusioned divorcee is likely to sit down in her frustration and bitterly lament the day she was ever carried away with the idea of being a homemaker.

NO VALUE?

These views of homemaking responsibilities can all too easily convey the impression that housekeeping is one of those sorry, dead-end occupations. I must confess I harbored vague ideas of the easiness of the task until my wife went overseas for a few weeks. By the time she returned, I was willing to admit I had completely underestimated the skills and energy required to keep up with a moderate-sized house and two kids. Of course, it is nothing like it used to be. I remember my own boyhood days and the way my mother slaved over the house. Washing day, for example, was quite an enterprise. All the dirty clothes were sorted on Sunday night and the decks cleared for the following morning. At the crack of dawn, we were filling the large container, called because of its basic material a "copper," with water, then building a wood fire underneath it. Dirty clothes were tossed in, to be periodically stirred with a clothes stick. Tubs of water were nearby, a wringer mounted on one side to remove the surplus water. Then the clothes went out to the clothesline to hang to dry in the breeze. All this is the prelude to the exhausting business of ironing. Small wonder one man of that day was offered a Monday off work by his boss and refused. His reason, "It's my wife's washing day, the one day I want to be as far away from the house as I possibly can."

The situation is different today. New materials have helped with the washing situation. One visitor from overseas was asked her impression of an American house and responded, "I wondered why so many houses had two bathrooms, but after being a houseguest for a week I understand. They have a second bath as a drying place for all their wash and wear clothes.

There are also new mechanical aids for all types of housework. One recent survey of American homemakers showed almost all the women owned a vacuum cleaner, more than 60 percent owned a dishwasher, half owned freezer, and over four-fifths owned electric blenders. Such an array of helps and gadgets should relieve the American homemaker of much of the drudgery of yesteryear. Perhaps it has complicated her life by using precious energy and posing problems of time and money when the complex machines break down.

Does all this mean a modern homemaker's skills are of little value? One interesting appraisal comes from an economist who works as an expert witness in court cases where the monetary value of a woman's work is being considered. After carefully analyzing a homemaker's work, he concluded it consisted of a multiplicity of tasks. He broke down the tasks of a full-time housewife as a cook, dishwasher, dietician, baker, waitress, nurse, chambermaid, buyer-shopper, veterinarian, laundress, home economist, seamstress, handyman, hostess, housekeeper, secretary, gardener, chauffeur, interior decorator, bookkeeper, ticket agent, and psychiatrist. If these services were to be duplicated, they would cost at least $14,500 a year.[3]

Superwife is the housekeeper par excellence, and one way she demonstrates this is "She gets up before dawn to prepare breakfast for her household" (Prov. 31:15 LB). In the time she lived, getting the household started probably required a lot of activity. The wealthy household employed domestic servants, but apparently superwife had a sense of responsibility and was unwilling to leave everything in the hands of the paid help. The majority of translations of this passage emphasize the early rising by translating the statement, "She gets up while it is still night." The statement fits in with the picture we already have of an energetic woman.

Of course, there are different rhythms in life. Some people are owls who like to stay up late at night and rise equally late in the morning. Others are larks rising early in the morning and probably retiring early at night. One woman I counseled was an owl, and her life rhythm became a problem in her housekeeping responsibility. Julia Posey told her story in a tired, flat voice.

I guess it just became a way of life. It seemed as if I had always to get up early. First, school days, in college I always had eight o'clock classes and when

I got a job I was constantly rushing to beat the clock. I worked in the early days of our marriage and an eager beaver supervisor had us breaking our necks to be at work on time. When I was pregnant with our first child, we decided I should become a full-time mother and one of the first real luxuries I experienced was not having set the alarm and jump up in the morning. Jeff was understanding and in the early days even brought me coffee in the morning. After the baby was born, we had some hectic nights and Jeff took his share of the getting up during the night and learned to slip out in the morning, leaving me to catch up on my sleep.

Following the baby days I guess it just grew into a way of life. Jeff arose in time to get to work, quietly slipped out of the bedroom, and went off to a short-order place for breakfast. He often jokingly complained about what he called "Joe's Greasy Spoon" and I would tease him by reminding him I wasn't a very good cook and if he really wanted it he could get up a bit earlier and fix his own breakfast. I slept as late as I could with a small child, stepped into my housecoat, and dilly-dallied around the house. When I was invited to some event being held in midmorning, I would make a joke of it, "Good heavens, no. I don't even get dressed until noon."

One day it began to dawn on me that this attitude of mine was not helping our marriage. I had become a "night person" I stayed up until all hours watching the late show and Jeff, who had to be up early, would be off to bed without me. Our love life was practically nonexistent. Then one day I accidently discovered he was having breakfast with an attractive divorcée who worked in his office. The alarm bells began to ring.

I decided the time had come for a change. In a long conversation I told Jeff I had realized I had gradually gotten into a sloppy way of starting the day and I was going to get up and fix breakfast for him. He told me it was not necessary. It certainly took some doing and I was often tempted to fall back into my old ways, but I got with it and life began to look different. This is the only time of the day that Jeff and I are really together and we can talk things over. I have been able to get my housework problem under control. No more housecoat syndrome for me.

Julia had learned a lesson, but she is only one among many. Even after years of marriage counseling, I never cease to wonder at the number of wives who are victims of the housecoat syndrome. When I call it to their attention, they look at me as if I am some old fuddy-duddy who needs to move into the seventies. Yet in this new era of married life in which husband and wife are partners, women will no longer be able to expect to wander carelessly into a new day while their husbands are rushing to meet business schedules.

I think I can identify with Julia Posey. I have never found it easy to rise early in the morning and often have the feeling I would dearly love to luxuriate in bed until later in the day. Breakfast in bed has always seemed pretty close to the ultimate pleasure. But such is my lot in life; with a hardworking husband who has a strange propensity for trying to beat the sun up in the morning. I have never been able to pamper myself. I have disciplined myself to be up at 5:45 A.M. for our nine-mile bike ride.

As I have worked in groups with women, I have been amazed at the number of wives who are willing to let their husbands either get their own breakfast or eat out somewhere. I see all sorts of dangers in this situation. Rising early calls for discipline, but it provides some wonderful possibilities.

The husband of a homemaker sees his wife as someone who takes her job seriously. If she does not find it easy to be up early in the morning, her willingness to make the effort shows her attitude of making a sacrifice to get the day well and truly underway.

Come eventide, a husband who has been working all day will feel more understanding about giving a little help to the household chores if his wife was up with him in the morning. If she was sleeping when he left, he will not be nearly as ready to pitch in and help when he is tired.

After years of exercising, I have discovered the biggest problem is regularity and continuity. Some research shows those who exercise early in the morning are the most consistent. A special project will more likely be done if you start it in the morning.

The comparison in your husband's mind between the gal who works with him who appears efficient, coiffured, and attractive when he arrives at work and you as a tired individual dragging around in a housecoat might not be too good.

Some nutrition experts believe breakfast is the most important meal of the day and necessary to get a good basis for the day's work. You will have provided a good nutritional start.

If you are careless about getting up, the image you present to your children may not be the best. Your daughter will not get a good idea about how a homemaker ought to function and your son will not know what to expect in a good, competent homemaker.

It will provide some spiritual opportunities. Jesus himself, "Rising up a great while before day went out . . . and prayed" (Mark 1:35). Asked the secret of his success, the famous black scientist George Washington Carver said, "I rise up early in the morning and go out into the woods and listen for the voice of God." I would not trade anything for the privilege of sitting hand in hand with my husband as we pray for God's guidance in the day we are entering.

THE HOMEMAKER EXECUTIVE

Readers of a previous generation split their sides over the antics of the Gilbreth family as recorded in *Cheaper by the Dozen*.[4] The main character in this rollicking story of family life is Frank Gilbreth, an industrial engineer and pioneer in motion study. An utter enthusiast, he applies his vocational skills to his own six boys and six girls. The results of this effort are hilarious. He arranges for his cameraman to make motion pictures of every facet of family life; and after examining the movies, he prepares plans of action that aim at saving time and energy. Record players were placed in each bathroom: he proudly boasts, "We are the only family in town with a victrola in every bath"; and language lessons in German and French play while the children brush their teeth and bathe.

When one of the children complains about the difficulty in changing records while in the bathtub, the irrepressible Mr. Gilbreth immediately turns his mind to the problem of bathing effectively and comes up with an application of motion study technique. He develops a way of placing the soap in his right hand, running from the top of the shoulder by a carefully planned route over the body outline to a circular rubbing movement on the stomach and finishing up with face and a final submersion in the bath.

A Better Way

Enlist the support of your family. Have a discussion period and seek the help and cooperation of all. You can decide on just how many tasks can be spread around.

Spend some time planning for each day. Write a list of tasks that are to have priority each day.

Go over your kitchen. Get it organized for efficiency. Try putting most frequently used appliances and food where they can be easily reached.

Plan menus ahead of time. This will help avoid monotony and make shopping easier.

Keep a shopping list handy. Write down what you need. Take the list to the store and save yourself from impulse buying.

Keep an eye on the utilitarian side of things. Buy easy-to-care-for items, like no-iron clothes, whenever possible.

Do some junking now and then. Have a garage sale. Call the Goodwill to haul away some of your surplus possessions. Get rid of the clutter.

Make sure you have a full load before you run your dishwasher or washing machine.

Parties need not be a big deal. One of the most gracious hostesses I know gives every arriving guest a card with a job on it. Mine was taking down the decorations after the party. I enjoyed it tremendously and got to know some nice people at the same time.

No aspect of family life or personal behavior is beyond organizing. An apple is totally consumed not from the side or "around the equator," as Gilbreth puts it, but starting at the "North Pole" and eating through the core, seeds and all to the "South Pole." As dishwashing constitutes a perennial chore, Mr. Gilbreth gives it special attention. He solemnly weighs whether it is better to stack the dishes on the table and carry a big pile or take them a few at a time and rinse while stacking. So the table is divided into halves, one half utilizing each method to provide data upon which to decide the most efficient technique. The twelve children are organized so an older one is responsible for a younger, and the irregular household tasks are awarded to the children on a low-bid basis so they can earn money and get the jobs done with maximum enthusiasm.

Although few of us would want to conduct our family life on such a basis, it certainly emphasizes the organizational aspect of life often overlooked in discussions of the family. Superwife, the subject of our discussion, was an executive, "She plans the days work for her servant girls" (Prov. 31:15). Any competent wife must be an executive.

CHAPTER 7

A Woman with a Green Thumb

 oing to inspect a piece of land, she buys it and plants a vineyard.

Prov. 31:16

ZAYIN

Visiting the nursery, I inquired of the gentlemen waiting on me as to the botanical name of a particular plant. He admitted his ignorance then added, "See if you can get hold of one of those garden club ladies; they sure know the botanical names of plants." Women and plants. Over four hundred thousand women who belong to garden clubs give evidence of the relationship. The first wife of recorded history was associated with the most widely known and celebrated of all horticultural enterprises—the Garden of Eden. Describing the setting within which God placed Adam and Eve, the Bible says, "Then the Lord God planted a garden in Eden and placed in the garden the man he had formed. The Lord God planted all sorts of beautiful trees there in the garden, trees for producing the choicest of fruit . . . a river from the land of Eden flowed through the garden to water it" (Gen. 2:8–10, LB). And again, "And look! I have given you the seed bearing plants throughout the earth and all the fruit trees for your good" (Gen. 1:29, LB). Thus began the association between wives and husbands and gardens that has continued across the centuries.

In Eastern countries, with their arid climates, the garden came to be particularly prized. As King Solomon accumulated more wealth, he became increasingly bored with the whole procedure. To indicate how wealthy and affluent he had become, he says, "I planted vineyards, laid out gardens and parks in which I planted all manner of trees, making pools to water my plantations" (Eccles. 2:4–6, MOFFAT). He was still dissatisfied even though he owned many gardens, which were the symbols of wealth and prosperity in his day.

Flowers and romance associate naturally. Scottish poet Robert Burns stated it:

> Oh my luv's a red red rose
> Thats newly sprung in June.

And in what is probably the most beautiful love song ever written (Song of Sol. 4:12–16), the bride is referred to as a garden.

BRIDEGROOM: *My darling bride is like a private garden, a spring that no one else can have, a fountain of my own. You are like a lovely orchard bearing precious fruit, with the rarest of perfumes; nard and saffron, calamus and cinnamon, and perfume from every other incense tree, as well as myrrh and aloes, and every other lovely spice. You are a garden fountain, a well of living water, refreshing as the streams from the Lebanon mountains.*

BRIDE: *Come, north wind, awaken; come, south wind, blow upon my garden and waft its lovely perfume to my beloved. Let him come into his garden and eat its choicest fruits.*

Within marriage, as in courting days, gardens were a concern and wives again evident. Take Jezebel, who is generally remembered for her painted face but who should be even more noted because of her husband and a garden. When she came upon Ahab lying on his bed, face to the wall and refusing to eat, like any conscientious wife she inquired as to the reason for this childlike behavior. He quickly responded that he wanted to buy Naboth's vineyard so he could make it into a vegetable garden, but Naboth refused to sell. In an overreaction to the situation, which may have been more a demonstration of her warped nature than of wifely devotion, Jezebel arranged for the murder of Naboth so Ahab could gain possession of the vineyard and build his vegetable garden. The garden in this instance came to represent the worst type of response a woman could make by fostering her husband's childish whim. In the New world, too, women and gardens have an association.

As the population spread across the country in the great frontier movement, women took their seeds and cuttings with them. Mary Riggs, wife of a missionary translator Stephen Riggs, traveled to South Dakota, where he began his translation work and she built a garden. She was later to lament, "The Indians and the babies, the chickens and the mice seen leagued to destroy the flowers, and they have well nigh succeeded."[1] Many endured the rigors of nature until one day while hanging out wet clothes in a bone-chilling March wind she contracted pneumonia. As her condition deteriorated, she fell into a delirium; and her last intelligible words were, "I have neglected the flowers."[2] A woman on the harsh and cruel frontier needed the tender touch of flowers to temper the rigors of pioneer life.

Superwife, living in ancient Palestine, would be interested to know her twentieth-century sister has maintained her horticultural interests. One beautiful example of this is a woman architect who specializes in skyscraper design. Those fingers pointing to the sky have something in common with the past in the form of "terrace gardens" adorning their upper roofs. This architect insists it is possible to grow in containers almost anything that grows in soil. Using containers, she has produced abundant crops. She sees other values besides fresh flowers or vegetables: "When the rest of the world is something I can't cope with, I turn to my garden." As if to confirm this feminine intuition, two men add their comments, "The garden is therapeutic for me"; "Gardening is relaxation and exercise combined." [3]

Gardening can strengthen a marriage, but it does not happen automatically. I am thinking of a couple named Owens. Following a highly successful career as an executive in a large company, Mr. Owens faced retirement with the same zest he had manifest in his successful business life. He went on a program of regular exercise, subscribed to all available magazines having to do with ranches and farms, and became very knowledgeable in agricultural pursuits.

When the Owenses moved into a rural area, one important part of their new home was a twelve-acre orchard and vegetable garden. Bringing his considerable abilities to bear on that garden, Mr. Owens produced an abundance of fruit and vegetables, so much, in fact, that they had no hope of ever using it all. They gave away much of the crop to friends, and, anxious that none of the produce should go to waste, they filled freezers, then began canning fruits and vegetables. Mrs. Owens, accustomed to gracious living, the literary society, her women's missionary organization, and the garden club, with its emphasis upon aesthetics rather than produce, began to feel she was now an unpaid canning factory worker. Casting her mind back to former days of freedom, she lamented, "When I married, I took my husband for better or for worse, not for lunch."

Nevertheless, a gardening enterprise involves many of the elements that go into a successful marriage. One couple reported a kindred interest of husband and wife in gardening. He grew vegetables; she grew flowers. As they labored in their respective areas, the spirit of competition grew. After some friendly disputes over fertilizing, they settled the matter by having "his" and "hers" compost heaps and entered into friendly competition as to whose was the biggest and best.

How well I remember the early days of our marriage, when in a burst of enthusiasm about being in our own little home and heeding the wartime propaganda about our patriotic duty to develop a victory garden, we perused seed catalogs, weighing the pros and cons of different plantings. Then we shopped around and accumulated enough seeds to plant a good-sized farm. Blistered hands, aching backs, and ruby red sunburn bore mute witness to our labors. The harvest brought delicious meals and gifts to incredulous friends.

We always maintained an interest in growing trees. My husband might well be called Johnny Shade Tree. Whenever we bought a house, we planted trees. In our first American home, we planted so many that a kid up the street, asked the location of our home, responded, "Go down the street till you come to the jungle then turn right." Shortly after we had moved to Fort Worth, Texas, which is located in prairie country, we were planting again. As our hobby mushroomed, we looked toward the piney woods of East Texas, where we managed to procure a piece of land, now a beautiful tree farm of thousands of well-ordered pine trees.

We love to wander around among the pine trees, feeling the snap of the needles beneath our feet and gazing incredulously at the rapid rate of growth. Like the poet, we feel again and again that only God can make a tree. In all the planning, purchasing, and working on our garden and later our tree farm, we have had a peculiar joy of being part of a shared enterprise.

The ideal wife of Proverbs 31, who showed her knowledge of soil and the value of land by buying a good piece of land and then working industriously planting a vineyard, would have enjoyed Katie Luther's company. The famous reformer Martin Luther set the medieval world on its ears when he, a monk, married Katie Van Bora, an ex-nun. Luther, himself a child of the soil, soon discovered his wife had similar interests, including farming. When in later life they acquired a farm at Zulsdorf, Katie took charge of the operation. On one occasion Luther wrote a satirical letter to her, "To the rich lady of Zulsdorf, Dr. Katherine Luther, who lives in the flesh at Wittenberg but in spirit at Zulsdorf." Referring to her in a letter to a friend, he said, "My Lord Katie greets you. She plants our fields, pastures and sells cows."[4]

Although Luther, who referred to the family as the "school for character," teased Katie about her love for growing things, he shared her interest and they divided their labors. He cared for the garden, where he grew lettuce, cabbage, peas, beans, melons, and cucumber; Katie worked at the orchard, where she kept them supplied with apples, grapes, pears, nuts, and peaches. Their common interest in gardening was yet another bond in their marriage.

Tennyson saw flowers and living plants as stepping stones to the knowledge of God:

> Flower in the crannied wall,
> I pluck you out of the crannies,
> I hold you here, root and all, in my hand,
> Little flower—but if I could understand
> What you are, root and all, and all in all,
> I should know what God and man is.[5]

In the simple flower lies much of God's majesty. Jesus said, "Consider the lilies how they grow: they toil not, they spin not; and yet I say unto you, that Solomon in all his glory was not arrayed like one of these" (Matt. 6:28). Of course, only those who are ready are able to apprehend the glory of it all, as Elizabeth Barrett Browning has said;

> Earth's crammed with heaven,
> And every common bush afire with God;
> But only he who sees, takes off his shoes.[6]

Life in eighteenth-century England was rough and brutish and the common people lived under appalling conditions, many finding escape in the gin palaces that promised, "Drunk for one penny, dead drunk for two." Recreational activities were few and a favorite spectator sport was the hanging of an unfortunate who fell foul of the law and went to his death in the presence of thousands of drinking, brawling fellow men. Pastimes included such cruel sports as bear baiting, hunting, and mutilating animals. All of this appalled John Wesley; and as people became Christians and joined his Methodist societies, he urged them to avoid the wicked and evil ways of the surounding society. To keep them from the Saturday night drinking orgies, he instituted watch night services to be held on Saturday nights. But what sort of activities would be available for them so that they could use their abundant energies? Why not gardening? He came up with the practical suggestion, "They may do it by cultivating and improving their lands, by planting their grounds, by laying out, carrying on, and perfecting their garden and orchards."[7] He spoke from experience and in his diary tells us that some of his highest spiritual moments came to him in a garden setting.

Among the lists appearing these days in women's magazines that assist the readers in their plant growing activities, one exhorted the reader to have the right attitude toward plants and "love them." That set me back and I queried a prominent psychologist who is also a plant freak as to what nonsense this was about loving plants. Without as much as batting an eyelid, he responded, "It simply means look at them, pay attention to them"; and in this sense it may be the plant lover has developed the skills of paying attention and caring that build relationships between people. And if we accept the tentative premise that flowers have emotional needs, it tells us something about superwife. The success of her gardening enterprise might confirm how unusually sensitive she was to others' feelings.

It is not without significance that in modern American cities, where the wide open spaces have long since disappeared, there should be a tremendous upsurge of women's interest in cultivating houseplants. Entering many a home today is like taking a trip down the Amazon River, with a great variety of plants growing from floor, wall, and ceiling, lying in wait to entangle the unwary visitor. The serpent in this Garden of Eden is often the supplier of the vegetation. In Arizona a special force is being set up to struggle with the problem of cactus nappers, who threaten to denude the countryside in order to provide plants for suburbia. Moved once, they might not be in place for very long as thieves go to work stealing hanging baskets and houseplants to be resold later at roadside stands.

The trouble many wives go to in an effort to have the best plants on the block staggers the imagination. Special banks of lights bring precisely the right degree and type of light carefully regulated to last a precise number of hours. The house must be kept at the correct temperature and exact degree of humidity. Some growers have special arrangements to catch unpolluted rainwater; others go through the process of distilling water to make sure it contains no impurities.

One woman told of a nightmare vacation involving a family automobile trip across the nation in which she, fearful of what might happen to her precious plants in her absence, carried her African violets so she could give them the attention they needed. After the trip her husband, weary and worn from carrying trays of violets in and out of motel rooms, delivered the edict, "It's African violets or me." Though she wavered a little in making her choice, she ultimately threw in her lot with her husband and turned her green thumb loose on other adventures. Busy at work with her watering, spraying, fertilizing, and cultivating, a modern wife is following the steps of superwife, who planted a vineyard.

CHAPTER 8

The Aerobic Glow

 er life is characterized by energetic hard work.
Prov. 31:17

HETH

Superwife was active. One description of her tells about the fine clothes she wore; and one translation of the verse we are considering is, "Strength is a girdle which she wraps around her body." This strength came in a large measure from her commitment to action. Just reading the description of all this woman's activities is enough to tire the more ordinary mortals among us.

There have been many speculations about the nature of women, including a woman is as she thinks, as she feels, and as she acts. Believing there is nothing more powerful than an idea whose time has come, propagators of the first idea take very literally the Bible statement, "As he [she] thinketh in his heart so is he [she]," (Prov. 23:7). Some years ago a man wrote a book entitled *Ideas Have Legs.* The thesis is that ideas are so powerful they translate themselves into action. Perhaps. Frankly, I am skeptical. If ideas have legs, many of those lower limbs are fractured, paralyzed, or crippled, for they travel no farther than the brief journey from the creator's head through his pen and stagger onto the paper, where for all practical purposes they give up the ghost and die. Although there is nothing more powerful than an idea whose time has come, if it remains just an idea, it will be stillborn. The idea must be translated into action.

There has recently been a belated recognition of the importance of feelings. One writer, citing the upsurge of sensitivity training groups, referred to it as "a revolution in feeling." Many theories of psychotherapy, convinced this is the area of greatest personality vulnerability, stress the emotional aspects of life. The emphasis on feeling is particularly heavy toward women, who are constantly told it is an essential part of their femininity. ("Women are more emotional than men.") So come the greetings: "How are you feeling?" "If I were any better, I couldn't stand it." "I feel like a million dollars." "I feel awful." "I wish I were dead." Many of these emotional experiences come to be so highly prized that people use drugs and alcohol to provide emotional highs and lows.

Visiting a department store where she had once worked for $10 a week, Joan Crawford, celebrated actress, met the clerk at the hosiery counter. The clerk lamented, "Gee, some people have all the luck." Crawford's "luck" was to be the product of a broken home, to have to work as a domestic helper in a private school where she was given broom handle beatings by the headmaster's wife, and to have to work for years in a theater chorus line. The clerk's words call to mind the maximum, "Success is luck—ask any failure." Joan Crawford got where she did by action. One writer notes that Crawford's credo was "Work, work, and more work." Even in her appearance, "Perfectly coiffured and meticulously made up, she made even beauty seem attainable through sheer determination."[1] Life consists of actions, behaviors. These behaviors give us a handle on life. We can take the initiative and do something about it.

The action premise, while acknowledging the potency of emotions and ideas, maintains that the most important factor in influencing human personality is what an individual does. The way women act determines what they learn. If it had not been for determined action by sturdy pioneer women, many of their sisters would never have been admitted into institutions of higher learning. It was widely thought that education was wasted on a woman, who would get married and become a housewife, a position for which education was considered unnecessary. But strong-willed women activists forced their way into medical and law schools and other educational institutions.

Apart from this unusual effort required of women, any learning implies action. We might have to change the statement "Ideas have legs" to "Legs give rise to ideas." An innovative psychiatrist named Dr. Low once said, "The humble muscles command as much dignity as the portentous brain cell. . . . The muscles are preeminently the teachers and the educators of the brain."[2]

The traditional way of looking at learning can be diagrammed as follows:

MASTERING MATERIAL → UNDERSTANDING →
CHANGES IN BEHAVIOR

This sounds good, but teachers often have students who carefully memorize material so they can repeat it on command. They cannot translate the theoretical knowledge into action, however. A more profitable way of approaching the subject might as follows:

DECIDE ON OBJECTIVES → PRACTICE NEW
BEHAVIORS → SATISFACTION → UNDERSTANDING

Action and learning go hand in hand. We have long known quiescent students do not learn very much. The learner must at least be *mentally* active if he or she is to learn. Now we are coming to see *physical* action may also be needed. Few countries have shown more ingenuity in their industrial development than modern Japan. Among the leaders of this new thrust is Tishiwo Doko, known for his dynamic leadership. Frequently described as a man of action, his favorite saying is, "Act instead of thinking it over. Only action produces ideas."

CONTROLLING TURBULENT EMOTIONS

When Henry Higgins, the tyrannical speech teacher in *My Fair Lady,* discovers Eliza has walked out on him, he launches into a long tirade, "Why can't a woman be more like a man?" As he calls off his chauvinistic list of women's weaknesses, he refers to Eliza "weeping like a bathtub overflowing" and presents the masculine stereotype of women as weeping, emotional creatures. Women have been taught to think of themselves in this way across the years; consequently, they may become the victims of a tyrannical emotional domination.

There was a time when a student of the human species would speak about the physical and emotional aspects of an individual as if they were discrete and separate elements. This is no longer done. A favorite word today among both the physiologists who study the body and the psychologists concerned with the mind is "psychosomatic." This word is made up of two Greek words meaning body and soul and is used to describe the close and intimate relationship between the body and the emotions. Psychosomatic is generally used to refer to the way the emotions affect the body. Investigators have discovered many people sitting in a doctor's office hopefully seeking medicine to cure their bodies have nothing really physically wrong with them. Their illnesses are sometimes referred to as "functional" or "psychogenic," implying the emotions have affected the bodily functioning. All too little thinking has been done about the reverse situation in the body-emotion relationship. One writer has suggested the word "somatopsychic" as a means of describing the influence of the body on the emotions.

THE ACTION PREMISE

One resident in a minimum-security prison noted a common attitude among the inmates. He observed how many of the men spent every available moment in bed, as if making an effort to sleep their lives away. One particular man caught his attention. He stayed in bed as long as possible in the morning; during lunch hour he sprawled on his cot; and as soon as he finished working at 4 P.M., he was off to sleep, only occasionally bestirring himself to read some pornographic material. The man walked more slowly every day. His shoulders became more hunched, and no emotion showed on his face. The observer also noted how many of the inmates were like zombies, walking in a daze, and, most significant, no one smiled.[3]

The realization that action affects our feelings has been one of the major factors in starting Americans jogging, running, swimming, and cycling as never before. Many women who initially thought these activities were distinctly masculine and watched their husbands begin to glow with health gradually realized they were missing out on something important, and they began to bestir themselves. One woman told of her growing interest. After a hesitating effort down the street during which males passing in their automobiles shouted some unflattering remarks at her, she decided to get underway within the shelter of her house. She worked out a route around the house that measured seventy-three laps to the mile and developed a strategy of changing direction every ten laps to keep from getting dizzy. Later she regained her courage and left the house, joining in spirit a large group of her jogging sisters scattered across the country, to go on a three-mile run through the streets. Another woman reports a daily mile-and-a half run not only makes her buoyant for most of the day but builds her self-esteem. She remarks, "I'm pleased with myself."

Just a few years ago the famous Boston Marathon was an exclusively male event, but now women are running the twenty-six-mile event and coming within thirty minutes of the male record for the race. And on the West Coast, a woman has shown what the "weaker sex" can do by winning the one-hundred-mile ultra marathon race.

Although most exercisers have undertaken their program in the hope of improving their health, many consistently report the activity gives them the feeling of euphoria. A professor of applied physiology has speculated as to what mechanism may be at work and comments, "I suspect the euphoria comes from emitting a lot of alpha waves, although there has been no study of it."[4]

One medical doctor reports on a number of patients involved in exercise programs. These people were in the program for physical reasons, but there was an unusual aspect in that almost all participants reported they felt better. The physician initially accepted these reports as indicative of superior muscle tone and physical condition but had a dawning conviction that the statements were indicative of a certain mental well-being. This phenomenon came to be referred to as "the aerobic glow."

Some researchers have become aware of the close relationship between physiological functioning and emotional reactions and the way superior cardiovascular functioning brings emotional benefits. One notes, "A person whose circulation has improved, giving his brain more oxygen and glucose is less depressed, less hypochondriac, will feel more alert, and is more ready to handle stresses and changes."[5]

Physiotherapists have been somewhat slow to utilize this technique in dealing with problems in the area of emotions. One report tells of psychiatrist Dr. John Greist at the University of Wisconsin, who treated fifteen cases of depression by prescribing exercise, specifically, jogging. The results were as good as or better than those obtained with traditional techniques. Another psychiatrist, University of Chicago's Dr. Jarl Dyrud, says, "One of the best ways of treating depression is by forcing activity. Of course, you have no way of telling which is cart and which is horse, but I have a hunch that a lot of this jogging exercise makes good sense as an antidepressant." In another instance, researchers from the University of Southern California, working with a group of men with anxiety-tension problems, found a fifteen-minute walk brought more relief than a mild tranquilizer.[6]

One of the most common reactions of emotionally overwhelmed people is to think of themselves as weak, tired, and having no energy. Because of this feeling, they generally take to bed to rest up and regain their energies. Many a doctor has aided and abetted the situation by telling the anxious patient to take it easy for a few days. Some research has shown this may be the wrong thing to do. It may only complicate the situation still further. They really need action.

Speech making is an anxiety-producing activity. Many a person who can carry on a conversation with one or two people in the most animated manner put before a group finds something strange happening. The tongue thickens, saliva dries up in the mouth, and the voice comes out strange and reedy. What is the best thing to do?

A man who listened to and criticized over one hundred and fifty thousand speeches in a forty-year period had an answer, "You are afraid to talk. You feel you will fail. You fail because you failed before, so you build a habit of failure." Dale Carnegie makes a suggestion to people who want to overcome their fear of speaking to a group. They should get a number of friends together and try talking to them. Little by little they will gain confidence from the success. Carnegie says, "Cure yourself of your fear of speaking by speaking."[7] Of course, he was repeating Emerson's maxim: "Do the thing you fear and the death of fear is certain."[8] In other words, by action you can change your feelings.

We might conclude that rather than a woman's life consisting of the way she feels or thinks, it is the way she acts. People judge us by what they see—our behavior—and this behavior in turn is the clue to vital living.

Complaints of women in the thirty-to-thirty-nine-year age bracket about being tense, moody, irritable, worrisome, weak, sensitive, and depressed have been noted by counselors. The complaints were so marked that investigators working in the Mayo Clinic prepared a scale on a personality test (the MMPI) and referred to the measurement coming from it as "the tired housewife syndrome." In discussing the uses of such a scale, some authorities noted it provides an excellent starting point for discussing emotional problems with women because "most women are quite willing to discuss tribulations specific to their role as a housewife." The obvious implication is there are great numbers of women ready to launch into a recital of how hard they have to work and the deleterious effects of all this labor upon them.

Descriptions of this syndrome seem to indicate that it really bears little relation to the amount of energy expended, and at least part of it may actually come from lack of activity. The housewife can order her working priorities more easily than most workers. Once she has her husband off to work and her children off to school, she is in a position to decide the order of the day's tasks. The simplest thing in the world for her to do is to slip back into bed for some more sleep. She easily falls into a self-defeating cycle, and we have a tired housewife in the making. As we noted earlier about superwife, she was up early in the morning to prepare breakfast and to plan the work for her servant girls. This may have been the secret of her unbounded energy.

Other Mayo Clinic data may provide at least a partial answer to the problem. A report from the Mayo Clinic tells of a rehabilitation program for heart attack patients. The major emphasis is on exercise. The natural tendency for a heart attack victim is to become skittish about any type of physical exertion. However, once these patients were launched on an exercise program, they not only improved physically but also emotionally. Researchers concluded, "All the test subjects had an increase in self-esteem and a more positive attitude towards their work and their disability." A Purdue University report states that sub-

jects who move into the higher fitness category achieve increased emotional stability, self-assurance, and self-sufficiency.

In our counseling center, we like to emphasize a statement made by E. Stanley Jones, "It's much easier to act yourself into a new way of feeling than to feel yourself into a new way of acting." Act good; feel good.

An ever-present temptation for a housewife is to opt for martyrdom. Poor me, the family dumps everything on me and here I am wearing my fingers to the bone. If I get feedback like this, I make a simple suggestion, "Whenever you are feeling put upon and worried that you are left with everything to do, just offer a little prayer, 'Thank you, Lord. This is going to do me good. The more I do, the better I will feel and the more energetic I will become.' "

CHAPTER 9

The Adventures of a Bargain Hunter

 n all her buying she carefully compares the available goods and watches for bargains.

Prov. 31:18

TET

When Tom Bullard had a heart attack and suddenly died, Mrs. Bullard's sister Alice flew in to try to comfort the distraught widow. With great difficulty, Alice finally got around to asking, "Now Gladys, I don't want to pry into your affairs; but I've been wondering how you are going to manage now that Tom is gone. Do you have an adequate financial basis from which to operate?" Mrs. Bullard burst into tears, "Oh Alice, I don't know. You know what a wonderful husband Tom was. He looked after all the financial matters of our family. I know you might find this hard to believe, but I don't even know how to reconcile the checking account. I just left it all to Tom. He wrote all the checks and paid all the bills."

Tom Bullard might have been a wonderful husband in many ways, but he made his wife into a financial illiterate. Considering that by the law of averages she was bound to survive him by approximately ten years, his "kindness" was actually cruelty. Every woman needs to develop skills in financial management.

Look at the virtuous wife. In this twenty-two verse poem at least seven verses mention some skill by the exercise of which superwife shows some financial acumen. The following stand out particularly clearly:

1. *Managing the household budget.* "Ever seeking to provide a varied diet for her family she purchases a variety of foods shipped in by importers" [v. 14].
2. *Investing the family resources.* "Going to inspect a piece of land she assesses it, buys it, and plants a vineyard" [v. 16].
3. *Comparison shopping.* "In all her buying she carefully compares the available goods and watches for bargains" [v. 18].
4. *Counseling the poor.* "Judging the indigent often to be deserving she works with her spindle to make clothes for them" [v. 19].
5. *Anticipating future contingencies.* "Looking ahead to the snowy days of winter, she has no fear, because she works hard in the summer and fall to sew scarlet clothes to keep her family warm in the winter months" [v. 21].
6. *Handling her clothing and household budget.* "Mastering the art of weaving she makes pillows and mattresses for the home and beautiful clothes for herself" [v. 22].
7. *Dealing with the traders.* "Operating a business she sews beautiful belted garments which she sells to Phoenician traders" [v. 24].

This wife of so many years ago had learned the hard way that she had to develop her money management skill if she was to survive among the sellers in the marketplace, haggle with the Phoenecian traders, or be financial counsel to the poor. What would she think if she stepped into today's society, with its credit cards, high-pressure promotions, telephone solicitations, TV commercials, coupon specials, and the thousands of inducements Madison Avenue has devised to separate housewives from their money?

Men who imagine women are incapable of managing family finances often have to learn the hard way that some wives can look after the economics of the home more effectively and efficiently than they. Martin Luther, the courageous man who withstood the wrath of the pope and resolutely defied Charles, the ruler of the Holy Roman Empire, did not do so well when it came to managing money. He married when he was forty-two, and his background as a monk left him indifferent to finances. He never made any money from the numerous books he wrote. If in the marriage ceremony he had said, "With all my worldly goods I thee endow," it would not have been much; for he was penniless.

Katie, having been a nun, had no money either; but she was at least conscious of the situation. She realized fiscal responsibility was not her husband's strongest trait. In a masterpiece of understatement, Luther once said, "I do not believe I can be accused of niggardliness." Katie found she was compelled to become the treasurer of the Luther household, which was no easy task. Her husband's continuing fiscal irresponsibility is shown in his statement, "I do not worry about debts because when Katie pays for one, another one comes."[1]

Katie went into action. She realized the only way to stop debts mounting was to increase the income and curb the spending. When Albert of Brandenburg presented Katie with a handsome present of twenty golden gulden, Luther suggested they send the money back; but Katie stubbornly insisted they keep it. She also put her foot down on her husband's generous gift giving. The banker Cranach joined forces with Katie by refusing to honor Luther's bank drafts. Then she turned an eagle eye on all her husband's activities. One letter to a friend indicated just how close Katie's surveillance could be: "I am sending you a vase as a wedding present. P.S. Katie's hid it." By her wifely devotion in the financial area, Katie made much of Luther's ministry possible. As Luther put it, "I give more credit to Katherine than to Christ who has done so much for me."[2]

WHEN A BARGAIN IS NOT A BARGAIN

A bargain is not a bargain if you do not really need the item, no matter how little you pay for it. I have a friend who has bought large quantities of merchandise he will never use. The last time I talked with him, he had just purchased two hundred prerecorded cassettes. His eyes glowed as he told me how cheap they were. When I responded that I failed to see how he could possibly use all these cassettes and asked why he had bought them, he said, "I am a sucker for a bargain." I fear he is just a sucker.

Then there are those remarkable women who get smitten with a disease more widespread at some times of the year than others—bargainitus. Molly Suskin was in a chronic condition. She was particularly vulnerable. Some people cannot resist alcohol, some tobacco, others dope; but Molly's weakness was more mundane. She just spent more money than the family finances allowed.

The word "bargain" did something to Molly. Whenever she saw an item "marked down," "reduced," "35 cents off," "usually $5.25 . . . now $3.95," it made the object highly desirable in her eyes. And as she continually overspent, her apparently mundane activities put increasing strains on her marriage. Indulgent at first, Tim, her husband, became increasingly exasperated at his wife's free spending attitude. He marveled at Molly's naive idea that whenever she bought something at a price lower than that for which it normally sold, she had saved money.

Tim came to dread Thursday evenings. Molly would systematically search the paper for the "weekend specials." He did not mind it so much on the groceries, but even in that department Molly could scarcely resist the temptation to overbuy the specials. What did they need with twelve cans of Alaskan king crab, the seafood-hating Tim asked himself. Molly began to resort to subterfuge. She developed all kinds of sneaky ways for covering her tracks so Tim would not know how she had spent the money.

After one painful episode in which Molly finally had to tell Tim about a $400 expenditure, he really got mad. In an effort to justify herself, Molly countered, "But, honey, it was such a good buy. I just couldn't pass it up." All effort at self-control abandoned, Tim replied, "A good buy, a bargain. I'm sick to death of having to spend money to save it! Who do you think you are? Mrs. Rockefeller? It's just getting beyond me. I work all the week and all I ever see is bills, bills, bills."

Molly, overwhelmed by Tim's intensity, dissolved into tears. Bargainitus can be a very dangerous condition. If not treated early, it can become a chronic disease, finally leading the victim into the bankruptcy or a marriage to its demise. Fortunately, it is a treatable illness; and the best therapy is indicated in our paraphrase, "She carefully compares the available goods and watches for bargains." An unneeded item is no bargain. It may be dirt cheap; but if you have no real use for it, it is expensive—very expensive.

Superwife bargained over many types of merchandise, but she was still a homemaker. When all is said and done, as an earlier statement in the chapter shows, she shared some of a modern wife's concerns: "Ever seeking to provide a varied diet for her family she purchases an assortment of foods shipped in by importers" (Prov. 31:14). She was apparently a gourmet cook and she spent a good deal of her time buying food.

Buying supplies might have been difficult for superwife, but it was nothing like the complex task facing a modern homemaker. In the days of the ideal wife, the products were in the marketplace for her scrutiny. Her modern sister has a much more difficult task, for food producers have learned not only to process and preserve food but also to package it. The perplexity of a modern woman is seen in a recent paraphrase of 1 Corinthians 13:2. "Though I have the gift of anticipating the good buys in the supermarket and understand all the mysteries of the differences of items that are the same weight even though disguised in jumbo packages. . . ." As this statement implies, grocery shopping can be a major problem for a modern wife.

The modern homemaker is caught in a perpetual round of visits to the supermarket. If there is one area in which she should be an expert, this is it. Yet suppose you walked into a supermarket one morning and someone stopped you and asked, "Will you please tell me what you plan to buy? What products, what brands, what quantities?" And suppose this same person stood at the checkout counter and made an item-by-item comparison of your actual purchases with your intended purchases. How would you make out?

If you are an average shopper, you would not make out well. Exactly 5,338 shoppers in two hundred and fifty supermarkets around the country were asked these very questions not long ago. The survey conclusions were surprising. Only three out of every ten purchases are firmly decided upon before the shopper gets to the store. The remaining seven are purchases resulting either from some vague advance plan or from a spur-of-the-moment decision. Almost half of all purchases are made completely on impulse. Two out of three shoppers never bother to prepare even a partial shopping list.

Remember that when you go shopping, you are always tempted to buy on impulse. Here are a few ideas to help you avoid doing so:

1. Set a shopping budget and stick to it.
2. Always make a list before you go shopping.
3. Be bargain conscious, but not at the expense of buying things you never use.
4. Do not be afraid to put things back after taking them off the shelf or to return them after buying them. The afterthought may be more worthwhile than the impulse.
5. Shop around and read the ads, but do not be bowled over by carefully devised sales lures.
6. Get what you really need, not what you think you might use someday.
7. Before you make a major purchase, think it over carefully. Try to hold off for a day or two.
8. Leave the children at home when you shop. Advertisers say children are great expediters of shopping impulses, especially in this TV age.

One popular definition of maturity is the capacity to postpone pleasure. If this is a valid concept, nowhere will a woman's maturity be more thoroughly tested than when she passes through row upon row of enticing goods that call for her to live today: "Eat, drink, and be merry, for tomorrow we starve." The ability to postpone the pleasure of making a purchase may in a large measure help keep harmony in her home and family.

BEST BUYS

The really sharp shoppers do a lot of comparison shopping and subscribe to such publications as *Consumer's Report* so they can evaluate the merits of various merchandise. One of the most valuable aspects of these publications is their list of items marked in some special

way as "best buys." The best buys listed in the book of Proverbs are
the following:

1. *Wisdom.* "Yes, if you want better insight and discernment, and
   are searching for them as you would for lost money or hidden
   treasure, then wisdom will be given you, and knowledge of God
   himself; you will soon learn the importance of reverence for the
   Lord and of trusting him. For the Lord grants wisdom! His every
   word is a treasure of knowledge and understanding" [Prov.2:3–6].
2. *Knowing Right From Wrong.* "The man who knows right from
   wrong and has good judgment and common sense is happier than
   the man who is immensely rich! For such wisdom is far more
   valuable than precious jewels. Nothing else compares with it.
   Wisdom gives: A long, good life, Riches, Honor, Pleasure, and
   Peace" [Prov. 3:13–17].
3. *Righteousness.* "Your riches won't help you on Judgment Day;
   only righteousness counts then" [Prov. 11:4].
4. *A Good Name.* "If you must choose, take a good name rather
   than great riches; for to be held in loving esteem is better than
   silver and gold" [Prov. 22:1].
5. *Humility.* "Better poor and humble than proud and rich" [Prov.
   16:19].
6. *Respect for the Lord.* "True humility and respect for the Lord
   lead a man to riches, honor and long life" [Prov. 22:4].
7. *Peace of Mind.* "Some rich people are poor, and some poor
   people have great wealth! Being kidnapped and held for ransom
   never worries the poor man" [Prov. 13:7–8].

These seven worthy investments can be acquired with little outlay of
money, although they will call for personal discipline and character.

A modern wife is subjected to modern financial stresses. These
pressures are so strong that it has been suggested the contemporary
marriage vow should be changed to read, "Till debt us do part."
Following the example of superwife as she watches for bargains and
carefully goes about her comparison shopping, a modern wife can avoid
this strain upon her marriage.

*Before we married, I had very little to do with money management.
The small amount I earned each week at my job I handed over to my*

mother. When we married, I found John generous with the salary. He just handed it over to me and told me to do what I wanted with it. Incidentally, he did me no special favor because it was rather a small salary in those days.

I had always dreamed of the time we would go shopping together, but John had lived in college dormitories for years and was unenthusiastic about shopping. When I suggested we go to the store and get some groceries, he quickly responded, "I'm afraid I'm not interested in grocery shopping. That's your department. Why don't you look after it?" So I was pushed into the position of purchasing agent for our family.

I have often found young wives do not like the responsibility of handling family finances and some go as far as to say, "If he won't accept his responsibility and look after the finances, I'm not going to bother with it." I do not think that is a good attitude. I soon learned some valuable lessons about handling money and I am grateful for the opportunities to do this. Wives usually outlive husbands and so should learn these money management skills.

When I read about the way the woman in Proverbs knew where true values lay, it reminds me of a story I read about an eighteenth-century divine. He had a large family and all his money was used to operate the church parsonage and buy food for his children. One night some of his recalcitrant political opponents set fire to his home. The house was soon in flames and the minister, his wife, and his family were fortunate to get away with their lives.

As the family stood watching the house burn to the ground, a group of church members and neighbors gathered around to commiserate. The minister called upon them all to gather around him and he said, "Come neighbors, let us kneel down; let us give thanks to God! He has given me all my eight children; let the house go: I am rich enough."

I am going to be a good steward of what earthly possessions God has given me, but I am not going to be a slave of mammon. Like superwife, I want to be sure I know where true values lie.

CHAPTER 10

Involved with Her Fellows

 udging the indigent to often be deserving, she works with her spindle to make clothes for them.

Prov. 31:19

YOD

Superwife worked deftly and skillfully with her hands. She washed the goat's hair, cleaned and carded the wool by piling it on a mat and snapping a bow string against the pile, and combed the flaxen fibers. Then she took her primitive spindle, a crude instrument about twelve inches long with a whorl of stone at one end to give momentum to its rotation, and spun the flax, wool, cotton, or goat's hair into thread. Martin Luther perceptively translates the statement: "She stretches her hand to the rock/ And her fingers grasp the spindle." It is a picture of busy hands, one whirling the rock flywheel, flying fingers at the other end of the spindle manipulating the thread. The work was long and tedious; but superwife did it, not because she had to—she was wealthy enough to employ servants to do all the irksome tasks—but because she wanted to. She was working at making clothes for needy people.

Superwife might have been the forerunner of the modern Goodwill center that takes the discards and repairs garments for the needy. One possible translation of the King James version, "Her hands hold the distaff," would be, "She repairs garments." Occupying such a position of influence, she may have called upon her friends and neighbors and queried them about their cast-off clothes. Once she had these in hand, she examined them carefully. When they needed mending, she repaired them.

Winding her way through Jerusalem's crooked streets, followed by servants carrying the products of her weaving and mending, she looked for the needy people. They were not too hard to find in that city of contrast between rich and poor. She talked with the poor about their problems and gladly offered the products of her work, hoping the garments would help to protect the impoverished wearers from the cold of a Palestinian winter.

The women of Israel may have been particularly concerned about the poor. Another famous woman, the redoubtable Queen Esther, was associated with a celebration of victory over a ruthless enemy; and one of the acts of celebration, perhaps at her insistence, was "Sending gifts to the poor" (Esther 9:22). In her childhood days superwife had been taught from the scriptures how she was to live with her fellow man, "If when you arrive in the land the Lord will give you, there are any who are poor you must not shut up your hand or heart against them" (Deut. 15:7, LB). Charitable institutions were nonexistent in that day, and these homegrown charitable enterprises may have been far more effective than some of the impersonal services available today.

CROWDED ISOLATION

I recently underwent surgery in one of our modern hospitals. Because I had a heavy lecturing schedule, I chose the slack Christmas period and decided to look upon the experience as a vacation. So I went first class—private room, complete with TV, telephone, and all conveniences. I soon discovered what modern technology has brought to a hospital stay. A host of technicians converged on me to conduct a variety of tests, catechize me with innumerable questions, and drain large quantities of my blood, leading me to feel I might at any moment need a transfusion and calling to mind Matthew 24:28: "Wheresoever the carcass is, there will the vultures gather."

Lying in my rail-enclosed bed like some animal on display at the zoo, clothed in a skimpy garment apparently designed by a man hater aiming to undermine the morale of any self-respecting male, I was alone once the vultures had departed. The closest thing to a fellow human being was a button I could press to gain access to the nurse's station. I had a vision of those nurses as I had seen them while on a trip to the X-ray department, sitting around, visiting, regaling each other with stories (probably about stupid patient antics), reading a book, or finding some other way to while away the time. When I made a bid for attention via the buzzer, a disembodied voice asked, "Can I help you?" But the intonation implied, "Unless you are at death's door, for goodness sake don't worry me."

Looking at the array of buttons, strings, and sundry appendages, I pondered my solitary situation, only to have my reverie interrupted by an aide who came to take my blood pressure. As he wrote down his figures, I sought to take advantage of the presence of another human being and asked him how high it was. The youth looked at me like I had attempted to borrow $20 and answered in a voice that indicated he had been listening to the nurses speaking to the patients, "I can't tell you." Having had my blood pressure taken weekly for some years, I threw down a challenge, "Whose blood pressure is it?" Whereupon the aide punished me by retreating, leaving me to my solitary confinement.

My mind went back to a hospital experience of many years previous when I was one of twenty patients in a ward. In the center of the ward, where she could see every activity of her charges, nurses, aides, and patients, sat the head nurse. Called sister, in this setting she was really a benevolent mother; and the patients in their carefully lined-up bed were her family to be cared for, lectured, fussed over, occasionally fussed at, and proudly displayed to their respective doctors as they came by. Woe betide any nurse, orderly, or other hospital employee who mistreated or neglected any of her "children." Sometimes it went to extremes, as when one sister decided to toilet train the whole ward, specifying certain times bed pans and bottles would be distributed to the patients. If a member of the community requested one of the items at any other time, the sister would give the offender a baleful look akin to that of a disappointed parent.

Here was an intentional community. New patients arrived and in short order we all knew about them, their ailments, famiiy, anticipated stay, and possible surgery. During visiting hours, relatives were introduced around and treats brought by a spouse or parents were shared with other patients. When someone lay seriously ill, other patients commiserated with loved ones. Hospital stays were longer in those days, and the walking members of the community pitched in and helped with the chores. At the foot of each bed hung charts, case histories, and such. These were surreptitiously examined by the ambulatory community members, and the information was passed on. Every crisis involved a good proportion of the ward.

When a patient was discharged, farewell celebrations were the order of the day. And that patient generally was not gone for too long. The ward had a faithful alumni group of ex-patients who returned, in one instance for years, to greet the new patients, regale them with stories of the past, recall personalities who had been there, and commend the skill of the staff. All of this was despite the fact that visitors had to pay a small sum of money to enter, which was, as a startled American friend remarked, "Rather like seeing the animals at the zoo."

Lying in my solitary bed in my modern, sterile room, I compared my hospital experiences. I now had the most advanced medical technology in the world working for me, but what I had gained in scientific skill I had lost in human relationships.

Superwife was vividly aware of the importance of relationships and the sense of isolation that came to that segment of society referred to as "the poor." One impoverished man reported that as he walked on the streets he heard footsteps of people either coming toward him or going from him; no one ever stopped. In ancient Israel, the division of poor and affluent was clearly marked. Superwoman belonged to the wealthy upper class in Jewish life and in part because of this may have felt a burden for the poorer people in her society. She not only felt; she did something, providing clothing that would bring a measure of self-respect and warmth to the indigent.

GIVING ONESELF

Israel, the scene of superwife's work, is the setting for people working to help others today. Modern Israel is facing problems quite different from those of ancient days. This ancient-new nation has absorbed about two million immigrants, over half of whom have come from the Middle East or the shores of the Mediterranean basin. The cultural backgrounds and experiences of these immigrants cause them difficulty in adjusting to this new democratic technological society.

Ironically, the Jewish society that originally propagated the basic principles of family life is experiencing difficulty in the area of home and family life. In an effort to cope with these problems, social workers are being trained in techniques of family therapy, an unexpected outcome of which is, "All graduates state that in their families there is more openness, more direct spontaneous and honest communication and that they are more able to express positive and negative feelings towards their spouses, parents, and children."[1]

All of this calls our attention to a note often heard in the teachings of Jesus. The Gospels record that on no less than six occasions Jesus made statements like, "Whosoever shall seek to save his life shall lose it; and whosoever shall lose his life shall preserve it" (Luke 17:33). Paul reminds us of a statement not recorded in the Gospels but carrying the same message, "Remember the words of the Lord Jesus how he said, 'It is more blessed to give than to receive' " (Acts 20:35). The evidence mounts to show that this is not only a spiritual legacy but also a psychological benefit to those who give themselves for others. John Bunyan put together a verse that contains the sentiment:

> There was a man,
> Folks thought him mad,
> The more he gave,
> The more he had.

This principle has long been known in the exercise of stewardship of people giving their money, but it applies even more in the lives of people who are willing to give themselves.

Superwife was in the vanguard of a host of women who felt concern for the less fortunate in society. One is Agnes Bojaxhiu, who sought to serve God by becoming a nun and went to India to work as a teacher in a girls' school. She became principal of Calcutta's Mt. Mary's High School, teaching the children of the city's wealthy families. But as she looked down into the nearby Noti Jeel slum, she had a growing conviction that she must give her life to serving "the poorest of the poor."

Other women joined Mother Teresa, as she is now known. To demonstrate their commitment and show it was possible to stay clean with a single change of garments, each woman limited her wardrobe to a pair of humble saris that cost only $1. Not permitted by her church to preach from the pulpit, she turned to preaching in the streets to the diseased and dying. She took literally the words of Jesus, "For I was hungered and ye gave me meat; I was thirsty and ye gave me drink; I was a stranger and ye took me in; naked and ye clothed me; I was sick and ye visited me; I was in prison and ye came into me" (Matt. 25:35–36). She sponged maggot-bloated wounds as if she were sponging Jesus' wounds.

This woman, who has worked among Calcutta's estimated two hundred thousand poverty-stricken people for twenty-seven years, reminds herself, "Loneliness and the feeling of being unwanted is the most terrible poverty."[2] Malcolm Muggeridge, the skeptic turned Christian, described his feelings as he put Mother Teresa on a train in Calcutta, "When the train began to move, and I walked away, I felt as though I were leaving behind all the beauty and all the joy in the universe. Something of God's love had rubbed off on Mother Teresa."[3]

As a girl, I worked in a mission in a slum in Sydney, Australia. The mission building had been donated by a long-departed benefactor. The conditions of the inheritance were simple, but one of them was to maintain the name of the building—"Consolation Hall." The name came from the idea that Christ was shortly to return and the building was a place where Christians would gather until that great day came.

Lovers of the Bible, the people who met and worked in the mission, felt one Bible portion more than another enshrined their hope. It was the statement, "For as often as ye eat this bread and drink this cup, ye do show the Lord's death till He come" (1 Cor. 11:26). They declared this hope with a prominently emblazoned segment on the front of the building, "Till he come."

The ragged urchins who roamed the streets read the passage somewhat differently, and they referred to the hall as "Tillie Kum," a title they rattled off with ease. The name confused local inhabitants and disappointed the workers in the mission.

Because we traveled a long way to get to the hall, we spent the whole of our Sundays there. Long, tiring days coming after a six-day week did not always inspire us. Nevertheless, I would be back again on the following Thursday evening to run a boys' club.

The children were poor, sometimes poverty stricken; and other agencies gave them clothes and food, but they did it in a somewhat impersonal way. We gave ourselves, spending long hours with them. As we watched some of those kids learn to hold their heads high, get an education and employment, and move out of the slums, we had the joy of feeling we were really involved with our fellows.

CHAPTER 11

The Hug of Life

nowing poor people need more than material gifts, she reaches out
both hands and touches them to indicate her compassion.

Prov. 31:20

KAF

From the discussion of superwife's manual skills as she works
with her spindle and needle to make and repair clothes for the poor,
the poem turns to the more psychological aspects of the act of giving
and tells how superwife expresses her concern for the poorer citizens
of Jerusalem. In the Hebrew the word "hand" is used twice in this
verse, and one scholar sees it as describing the way a gift is given with
an open hand. However, most scholars favor the idea that this verse
refers to a gesture of compassion, apart from any gift. Superwife is no
mere do-gooder, aloofly handing out material gifts; she also gives part
of herself.

Hands are often the vehicles of personal concern. Students of communication have long noted the importance of nonverbal communication, and some have referred to what they call "body language." No
part of the human body is more communicative than the hands, particularly in greeting. An Indian friend of mine greets me by placing his
hands together in an obsequious prayer attitude that seems almost
blasphemous and bothers me.

I am a product of a society that prefers the handshake as a method
of greeting. But even handshakes come in a wide variety: the strong,

firm bone crusher; the flaccid, dead fish that flops into your waiting hand; the politician's handshake, in which the shaker grasps the sha-kee's right hand then cups it with his left hand; or shaking the right hand while grasping the shakee's forearm or right shoulder with the left hand. Although the last procedure is acceptable with two dear friends, many people feel it is insincere or falsely ingratiating.

Women greet each other in a slightly different manner, but it can be just as lethal as the most rugged bone crusher. I shall never forget a sweet little lady who took hold of my left hand in her right and squeezed it with unbelievable force, causing my wedding ring to bite into the joint of my little finger and leaving me in pain for weeks afterwards. One peculiarity of women is the way they use their hands in expressing their feelings to each other, particularly in a crisis. Instead of shaking hands, they reach two hands toward each other, gently taking hold of both hands with appropriate concern expressed on their faces. They may move from this to an embrace. Our verse has in it just this idea; "she reaches out both hands" to the poor and needy.

The Heimlich maneuver, named after Dr. Henry J. Heimlich, a Cincinnati surgeon, is a technique to prevent a person from choking to death on a piece of food or foreign object that has "gone down the wrong way" and blocked off the trachea. The maneuver calls for the helper to stand behind (it can be done by kneeling astride) the choking individual and using one hand to push the other fisted hand sharply into the victim's abdomen just below the rib cage. The air pressure pushes the obstruction from the windpipe, rather like a cork being popped from a champagne bottle.

Records indicate that as many as seven hundred and fifty persons have been saved by this maneuver, and it is now being used to force water from the lungs of drowning victims. Because of its effectiveness, the technique is being widely used in schools, industry, and the armed forces. Its popular name is the "hug of life."

Of course, the hug of life, in the best sense of the phrase, is much more than an emergency procedure for choking people and applies to all stages of human growth and development. It starts in babyhood. A mother carries her baby within her body and birth brings the crucial moment of separation. Some psychologists refer to this experience as "birth trauma" and say it may be significant for the rest of one's development. It has been claimed that if a baby is separated from its mother for any significant period of time during the first two years of its life, it may suffer from "maternal deprivation" and be irreparably damaged.

Although ideas like this were in vogue just a few years ago, they have been gradually abandoned or ignored. Now has come a reaffirmation of the principle from such a stuffy institution as the American Medical Association, which has given its official blessing to the practice known as "bonding." The procedure runs counter to today's general practices, in which mothers give birth to their babies in antiseptic surroundings and the baby is immediately taken off for cleaning and placement in the nursery, where it can be viewed from a distance behind protective glass.

Bonding involves taking the newborn child, not even washed off, and putting him or her into the mother's arms. Mother and child spend a few moments together in skin-to-skin, eye-to-eye contact. Over seventy years ago a noted French doctor, Pierre Constant Budin, noted that mothers and babies interact better if they are not separated at birth. Now even the AMA encourages bonding.

A MODERN JEWISH WIFE

Superwife, with her belief in the efficacy of reaching out and touching needy people, would have been proud of her twentieth-century successor in modern Jerusalem. What superwife was to the Jewish community in Old Testament times, Golda Meir became to present-day democratic, technological Israel. She shared with superwife a belief in the efficacy of a compassionate touch. This was demonstrated during an interview between the daughter of an American president forced into an ignominious retirement and the Israeli prime minister, living in the honored autumn of her distinguished career.

As Julie Nixon Eisenhower concluded her interview with Meir, the redoubtable leader suddenly switched roles and became the interviewer. She asked, "How is your father; is he writing every day? What is he doing now?" Julie suddenly lost her composure; her voice broke; and tears flooded her eyes. She could not speak. A few minutes later the interview concluded and Julie moved toward the door. The prime minister impulsively reached over and hugged and gently kissed her interviewer. Julie remarked about Golda, "Her answer to the vicissitudes of life is compassion not words." Like superwoman, Golda showed her compassion by physical contact.

As a footnote to the Julie Eisenhower-Golda Meir incident, we might note the older woman reached down to the younger; but the biggest problem may be just the reverse. It is easy to hold a pretty body, a firm-fleshed child, a young person blooming with physical well-being; but they do not need and in fact often care little about physical contact. Those who need it most are the elderly, the unattractive. A recent picture of an old woman in a St. Petersburg, Florida, park showed her with hands full of grain and pigeons resting all over her head, shoulders, and arms. She was willing to spend her meager resources on feed to gain the birds' company. What a potential helping situation for some concerned human being.

Drug addicts are probably the most difficult people of all to try to help. A major difficulty is the "code of the streets," an attitude that causes the addict to see society as divided into two groups: "we"—the addicts—and "they"—the establishment. The ruling principle becomes "Thou shalt not squeal," which keeps the "we" from becoming friendly with the "they."

Working with a group of addicts, I was constantly frustrated by their implication or outright assertion, "It's us against you." Then came a breakthrough when some of the group began to level with me. After one such session, the men lingered after the time for departure; and when they finally left the room to go back to their wards, the chaplain said, "You've finally got through to them." "How do you know?" I asked. "Well, after the session concluded, each of the men came up and touched you. That's a good sign as to how they feel about you." The touch of the addict's hand is his gesture of encouragement. Once familiar with it, I always knew when things were going well in my relationship with them. The touch was of the greatest significance.

As psychologist Sydney Jourard says, "Large numbers of people are virtually untouched and out of touch. Others are touched, but only with the intent of sexual arousal. This contact can be unaffectionate and even hostile. What people need—both children and adults—are warm handshakes, pats, and hugs that indicate the other person is giving affection and esteem. In a society where there is little touching our bodies tend to disappear. We lose the capacity to experience our bodies as vital, enlivened and as the centers of our being."[1]

TOUCH IN CHANGING BEHAVIOR

Hands may play a large part in changing behavior. The traditional way of doing this has been using hands to punish; our language is replete with expressions, "box his ears," "spank him," "slap her fannie." Each of these emphasizes the negative aspects of discipline by trying to persuade the individual not to repeat a behavior. But the word "discipline" means to teach, and the best way of teaching is to ignore unwanted behavior and commend and reinforce desirable actions.

Many mothers become expert in using their hands to reinforce desirable attitudes and actions. Watch an astute mother as her child comes in promptly from school and she hugs her in her arms; or as her little boy struggles to hold back a tear while the doctor is giving him a shot and mother strokes his hand or arm; or as she takes her little son for his first day at school, gently but firmly holding his hand; or when her daughter finishes a difficult assignment and she pats her on the shoulder, arm, or head. It may be we have gone about discipline in the wrong way. Perhaps it has been administered at the wrong place and in the wrong manner. Rather than a paddle to the bottom, it should be a touch or pat to the head.

THE HEALING TOUCH

These considerations of the persuasive power of touch lead us to a new look at the time-honored practice of laying on of hands. The Christian church has made the laying on of hands a part of its practices and ceremonies. Roman Catholics and Episcopalians see in it the symbol of apostolic succession. Some nonliturgical churches use the practice in ordaining ministers and deacons. Jesus Christ used the laying on

of hands with sick people, even touching the most repulsive of all
people, a leper; and it became an accepted method of healing.

Belief in the healing power of touch goes back to the dawn of history.
An Egyptian papyrus dated before 1500 B.C. tells of healing ceremonies
that involved the laying on of hands. In England it was touching by the
king, a practice that started with Edward the Confessor. The sick
kneeled before the king, who touched them while his chaplain intoned,
"He put his hands on them and healed them." The custom was passed
on by the royal line. King Charles II is said to have touched nearly a
hundred thousand people. Queen Anne was the last of the British rulers
to practice the "king's touch." One of the celebrated people she
touched was the infant Samuel Johnson in 1712. Boswell tells us that
Johnson's mother took him to be touched on the advice of the family
physician; but it was to no avail because he was not healed.

The custom spread to the Continent and was practiced by many of
the French kings. Not all rulers were convinced, however. William of
Orange considered the practice a mere superstition, and he only
touched one person. During the process he muttered, "May God give
you better health and more sense."

A rather unusual confirmation of the validity of touch, the evidence
of relationship, as a factor in physical health has come to light through
the work of a psychologist. Dr. Lynch noticed how loss of contact with
their fellows affects physically ill persons. He noted that single, widowed, and divorced people are much more prone to disease than married people. Widows between the ages of twenty-five and thirty-four
have a fivefold higher coronary disease rate than married women in the
same age group; divorced people are twice as likely to develop lung
cancer or suffer a stroke. The message, according to Lynch, is that
loneliness kills. "Loneliness is not only pushing our culture to the
breaking point, it is pushing our health to the breaking point."[2]

Lynch makes an eloquent plea for recognition that social isolation
leads to emotional difficulties and ultimately physical deterioration and
that family and social life are just as important to physical health as diet
and exercising. He suggests physicians may need to realize their bedside
manner might be more important than the pills they prescribe. One
study showed that petting could produce profound effects on dogs'

cardiovascular systems and that even people in comas show improvement when doctors or nurses hold their hands.[3] Physical contact carries a message.

I once served as chaplain of a large army hospital where we had a fine dermatologist of Polish origin and training. While I was on rounds with him one day, we stopped before a bad case of dermatitis. The nurse removed the dressings to show the badly infected skin. Without a moment's hesitation, the dedicated doctor leaned over and began to rub his fingers over the infected spots. The onlookers were amazed, as was the patient. Smiling into the patient's face, the dermatologist assured him that everything was going to be alright. Back in his office later, I asked the doctor if it was his usual practice to touch the infected spots. He replied that in his medical training he had been taught never to show fear in the presence of infection. He claimed a confident attitude helped quell the patient's apprehensions. It could be that laying on hands helps break down the isolation sickness sometimes brings.

Among the strange by-products of Christianity, none is more controversial than the work of "faith healers" who conduct meetings at which sick people are invited to step forward and be healed. Many of these preachers claim to have a "healing right arm" and say that from it comes a feeling, "like an electric shock," that goes through the subject, who may or may not feel it. In some sense everybody has a "healing right arm." When we reach out toward people to help them, we often, by means of our arm, bring healing to them. Like superwife, we may need to learn the lesson of the power of touch. We have far too long seen physical contact as sexual; we may need to learn that touch used with the elderly, the poor, the young, and the unattractive can be redemptive.

One high moment in my life came when I met Dr. F. W. Boreham, the famous essayist. This unusual man, who wrote approximately forty books of essays, was to speak at a conference in which we were involved. Dr. Boreham had little use for many modern amenities. Living in a nice home, he had no telephone; it interrupted too much, he said. He did not use a typewriter; it is too mechanical. He wrote his essays in longhand; sent them to a paper, which printed them; cut out the pages and stuck them in an exercise book; and when he had enough, mailed them off to his publisher, who created a book out of them. He did not drive a car, preferring to walk, cane in hand. Dr. Boreham was the perfect English gentlemen.

The leaders of our conference ask John and me if we would pick up Dr. Boreham for his speaking engagement. What a delightful experience it turned out to be. Dr. Boreham was a charmer. And when he spoke to a great assembly of youth on the word "add," the words flowed out of him as he painted verbal pictures that captivated and enthralled his listeners.

As we drove back to his home, we felt we wanted to linger along the way and prolong the experience. He had recently announced he was not going to write any more books; but as we quizzed him, we discovered he was in fact writing yet another volume entitled I Forgot to Say.

John insisted on taking our picture. I stood, my arm proudly through Dr. Boreham's and he squeezed in closer. We got in the car and all the way back to his house he gently held my hand in his as he shared his wit and wisdom with us. The gentle touch of his aging hand was a benediction. His touch was as gentle as the beautiful essays he wrote.

When I conduct sessions of experiential Bible study with husbands and wives, part of the procedure is to have husbands and wives tell each other one thing they particularly like about each other. Then I have them embrace. That embrace after they have spoken so warmly to each other seems to bring out something and the tears frequently flow.

Jane Howard in Please Touch recounts her experiences in sensitivity groups. She calls attention to the lengths people were willing to go in order to have a closer relationship with other people. She notes the results were not always the best; in fact, some of them were downright humiliating and might have destroyed one person's faith in another.

In a new book, Howard suggests how the benefits of family life can have a resurgence in our day and extols the merits of "surrogate families," that is, families in which people choose who will be their relatives. We have been advising adoptive parents to make their adopted children feel better by telling them they are "chosen" children. Why not apply the same principle to providing family experiences?

As Howard develops her criteria from chosen families, she comes *upon the subject of showing affection and quotes a woman who calls these intentional families "tribes." She says, "The tribe that does not hug is no tribe at all. More and more I realize that everybody, regardless of age, needs to be hugged and comforted in a brotherly and sisterly way now and then, preferably now."* [4] *I could not agree more.*

CHAPTER 12

Planning Ahead

 ooking ahead to the snowy days of winter, she has no fear, because she works hard in the summer and fall to sew scarlet clothes to keep her family warm in the winter months.

Prov. 31:21

ל

LAMED

Busy at work in the oppressive heat of a Jerusalem summer, superwife looks beyond the discomfort of the enervating days to motivate her family to think on toward the winter. Lethargic servants and family members found it difficult to share her enthusiasm as she urged them to work hard at burning wood for charcoal that would take the chill off cool evenings later in the year and preserving food to be stored for the winter months. But she would not trust the responsibility for the clothing to anyone else. She worked diligently at weaving and sewing.

She sought out a cooler place in the house and periodically fanned herself in an effort to cope with the summer heat but continued on busily plying needle and thread. She remembered the bone-chilling winter of previous years, when in their inadequately heated home the only way to ward off the cold was to wear warmer clothing. As she shopped in the marketplace, she looked around for a special material, referred to in the statement, "All her household are clothed in scarlet" (Prov. 31:21). This was probably a special red woolen material that may not have been much warmer than other types of wool, but on snowy days the blazing scarlet contrasted so vividly with the snow that it *felt* warmer.

Another way of translating the Hebrew word would be as "double garments" ("All her household are clothed in double vestments" [SPURRELL]). This has led to the conclusion that superwife made numbers of garments that would fit on in successive layers. It is interesting, considering the finding of skiers and others who endure the rigors of the snow and cold weather, that the most effective way of keeping warm is to put on successive layers rather than just one thick garment.

The most important point is not so much the type of clothing but rather superwife's state of mind. She made a deliberate decision about what she would do in preparing for the winter, still months away. Because of this decision, she has a quiet spirit. "She has no fear"; she is "not afraid of the snow" (Prov. 31:21). Indecision and uncertainty can be twin torturers that keep their subject on a constant rack of punishment. As one mother put it, "I know I should do something but I am bogged down forever worrying whether it makes sense to do anything." In these situations the worst thing a woman can do is to do nothing.

Stop for a moment and ask yourself how you make decisions. Five possible ways follow:

1. *Habit.* There are certain routines you go through. As the situations arise, you automatically go through these because you have always done it this way. You do not stop and ask yourself if there is a more effective way of approaching the problem. Such an attitude reminds me of the word of the formula, "As it was in the beginning, is now, and ever shall be, world without end, amen."

2. *Others' demands or requests.* You get the feeling all your life is decided by others, your husband, your children, your friends. You are just a reactor to their requests. You spend your life doing what others want you to do.

3. *Inaction.* You say to yourself, "One of these days I am going to learn to play tennis, write an article, learn to type"; but these forever remain vague dreams. Dreams are important and help keep us from being trapped in a limited world and limited experi-

ences if, as Kipling put it, "you can dream and not make dreams your master."[1] Translate your dreams into action.

4. *Spur of the moment.* You rationalize and say, "I just hang loose; when a situation arises, I take it in my stride." Or you may make it sound even more respectable by saying, "I live a day at a time." In actual fact this means you do not bother to make any decisions that concern the future.

5. *Conscious decision.* You consider all the alternatives, try to predict the outcome, and commit yourself to a line of action.

Some of these methods are alright. Habitual choices keep the necessary routines of life going; a spur-of-the-moment decision may have creative possibilities; some decisions made in response to the demands of others may be an essential part of any cooperative venture; and every one of us is entitled to a few daydreams. However, the best type of decision is one consciously and deliberately made.

Of course, this does not mean once a decision is made it is irrevocable. Phyllis and Joanne are both amateur photographers. Phyllis constantly wins prizes with her pictures, but Joanne's acquaintances dread her slide shows. It is not that Joanne does not try; she is painfully careful, getting the right angle, the correct pose, the desirable light. When everything is just right, and only then, does she click the shutter, just one shot, no sense wasting film.

Phyllis does not go to quite the same lengths as Joanne; but when she begins to shoot, she fires off her shots as if the camera were a machine gun. As she uses a roll, she gleefully reloads to start at it again. When Joanne's pictures are processed, she keeps every one as though it were a treasure. Phyllis is just as willing to throw away her pictures as she was to snap them. Any shot not up to standard is discarded. As she discards, she learns, not that way again. That is how decisions should be made. Each decision is tentative and open to reassessment.

In making these decisions as to what we are going to do, we should bear in mind the "80/20 rule," which is, "If all items are arranged in order of value, 80 percent of the value will come from only 20 percent of the items; and the remaining 20 percent of the value will come from 80 percent of the items." This rule is not precise; sometimes the proportions change a bit. In any list of ten items, doing two of them will yield most of the value (80 percent). Here are some examples:

80 percent of the dinners are prepared from 20 percent of the recipes

80 percent of dirt is on 20 percent of the floor most frequently used

80 percent of the dollars are spent on 20 percent of the meat and grocery items

80 percent of the washing is done on the 20 percent of the wardrobe that consists of the well-used items

80 percent of TV time is spent on 20 percent of the programs most popular with the family

80 percent of reading time is spent on 20 percent of the pages in the newspaper

80 percent of the telephone calls come from 20 percent of all the callers

80 percent of eating is done in 20 percent of the favorite restaurants

The important thing is to find the most important things and decide which we will do, leaving the others undone.

What sort of planning does today's homemaker need to undertake? It would be a good idea for her to take a long look at her goals in life. This can be accomplished by asking the following questions:

1. What are my long-range goals? What do I want to accomplish in life?
2. What do I hope to achieve in the next three years?
3. Suppose I knew I would be killed in an auto accident in six months. What would I do in the intervening time?

Begin with your lifetime goals. Let your imagination run wild. After you have them down, select the top three, listing them as A1, A2, and A3. Do the same with your three-year list and your six-month list. Remember, none of these is static but open to change at any time.

Establish the ABC priority system. In any list of activities, some will be of more value than others, as we have already noticed. Place the letter A alongside those of high value, B alongside those of medium value, and C alongside those of low value.

To handle this situation, we must continue to break our time into increasingly smaller segments. A well-known author who has written more than twenty-five books seemed to live such a busy life that it would be impossible for her to have enough time to do her writing. Her secret was she did not anticipate long periods of work time. She used small segments of time, waiting at the airport, on the airplane, and between appointments. I remember reading about an author who lived at the time of the French Revolution. His room overlooked the square where the guillotine was beheading people, but he only occasionally looked out on the excited crowd. He continued to give himself to his work. It is this sort of discipline that gets things done.

The problem is aggravated for a housewife. It sometimes seems she is on a twenty-four-hour schedule. She has a series of deadlines; getting the kids off to school, preparing meals, buying and laundering clothes, attending club meetings, picking up and delivering the kids, taking a course at the community college, buying the groceries, and looking after the house. All of this means a housewife, of all people, must learn to schedule her time.

A wise homemaker uses her waiting time. While in Japan I was amazed at how the Japanese utilized every spare moment. A ride in the bus or subway was a study in concentration; most of the passengers sat with their heads buried in books. Many a homemaker is frustrated by time spent waiting, such as for the children after school or little league. Take a book along; itemize the budget; prepare the invitations for the party or other social event. Have some type of a carrying case for books or work to be done.

Speaking of Japan brings to mind a Japanese ruler and an Australian university professor. The Japanese ruler is the mythical mikado in Gilbert and Sullivan's musical comedy of the same name. Mikado joyously sings, "I have a little list," and proceeds to enumerate all the poetic justice he has been able to devise as punishments for those people who annoy their fellows. His list, not its contents, reminds me of the Australian professor.

As a student at the University of Sydney, I had the respect for professors so often found in European type universities. On one of the few occasions I ever got to visit with one of my professors, I could not help but notice a list on a piece of paper headed "jobs for today." Herein may have been one of the secrets of his success. Every woman needs such a list of priority items.

Another secret of getting a lot done is learning what *not* to do. Too many homemakers complain, "I work hard. I never stop from morning to night, yet I can't get all my work done." The problem is frequently not the amount of time spent but the activities on which the homemaker focused. Less important than how much time was spent is what was done. Far too many housewives are conscientiously working long hours at tasks not worth the trouble.

If a woman is to get some time for a special project, she must plan her time. Planning means she will decide on a priority item, place it on her schedule, then plan her other activities around the special event. Suppose she wants to take a course in painting. Having learned the course is taught on Tuesdays from 10 A.M. to 2 P.M., she plans her week accordingly. She makes arrangements for the children and goes to her class no matter what condition the house is in. Another wife and husband decided they needed some time together, so they made a definite supper date for each Thursday and arranged Thursday's activities around their date. The husband was much in demand as a speaker; so to avoid a conflict, he wrote his Thursday night date into his schedule.

The main problem with planning seems to be that many women have the idea it means sitting down and looking into space, *thinking.* But planning involves *action,* in the first instance, writing it down on paper. Then try out the plans. After trying out the activities, evaluate them before making a new effort.

One of the characteristics that differentiates human beings from other animals is our capacity to anticipate the future. In her study of outstanding personalities, Dr. Buhler concluded human lives are characterized by directionality. We set up goals and moved toward them by orderly steps. Dr. Gordon Allport took note of these studies and postulated directionality as a test of the mature personality.[1] By this standard, superwife was the quintessence of maturity.

CHAPTER 13

Clothes Make the Woman

astering the art of weaving, she makes pillows and mattresses for the home and beautiful clothes for herself.

Prov. 31:22

MEM

If, as popular folklore has it, primitive man and his mate lived in a darkened cave, there is a good chance that on a snowy, cavebound winter day she announced that as soon as the weather warmed a little she intended to move the fire to another corner of the cave and suggested that as soon as he could get to moving around the countryside again he find some petrified wood for a table. And while he was about it, why not keep his eyes open for a beaver or two. She was sick of wearing these old rabbit skins. Thus perhaps at the dawn of history a woman was concerned about dressing her house and herself. Home decorating and clothing have long been a concern for women. Proverbs 31:22 indicates superwife could have been a bridge between primitive and modern woman.

DRESSING YOURSELF

Dress may communicate in many ways. The classical Japanese theater, known as the Nō Theater, leans heavily upon the actors' costumes. These garments are painstakingly made, with weavers working for as long as a week to complete six inches of the garment. It takes as much as a year to prepare the material for the type of tie-dyeing they use and another year to unpick the material. Plays are acted on a bare cyprus wood stage, so the actor's robe is both the costume and the set. Design motifs in the material set the mood for the play.

Apparel certainly emits signals, but be careful how you interpret those signals. A Wisconsin judge, in reaching a doubtful verdict in a rape case, said, "I'm trying to say to women, stop teasing. There should be a restoration of modesty in dress and elimination from the community of sex gratification business."[1] The result was the first judicial recall election in three decades. A woman won the new election. It turned out she had a sister who had been raped some years earlier. Although the whole unfortunate episode became a battle over women's rights, it should have been possible to point out women's responsibilities. Dress is frequently used for sexual invitations, and women should be aware of the message they communicate.

Her dress may have communicated a message for Narcissa Whitman of New York state, who in 1839 offered herself for service as a missionary in the Oregon Territory. Before embarking on the hazardous six-and-a-half month trip across the country, Narcissa married a physician named Marcus Whitman. Her wedding dress was of black bombazine and the whole family was similarly dressed in a somber hue. Some have suggested it was probably the best dress she owned; but from what we know of the widely accepted idea that religious commitment in that day meant an end to fun and formality, the bride and her family's black clothing may have carried a special message of commitment to her serious mission.

One researcher has tested the theory that dress affects human relationships. The experiment involved traveling between two cities about a hundred miles apart. On Monday, Wednesday, and Friday, he wore old jeans, sandals, and a multicolored sweatshirt. On Tuesday, Thursday, and Saturday, he dressed in a clean, pressed shirt, neat pants, and shined shoes. Each day he went out to the highway at the same time and stood in the same spot, signaling with his thumb in the same way. The only difference was his clothes.

On Monday, Wednesday, and Friday, he was offered rides in nondescript vehicles driven by people dressed much like him. Clad in his dressier clothes, he got rides in shiny vehicles driven by well-dressed people, some of whom remarked how nice it was to see a young person nicely dressed. Dress gives a nonverbal message and many people do not realize just what the message is.

Superwife dressed particularly well. Her attire was expensive. Two descriptive words in Proverbs indicate her clothing was linen cloth and the color was red purple. The most valuable purple garments were brought from Tyre and Sydon. Not only did superwife buy food imported by ships, but she dickered with traders over their expensive material.

DRESSING YOUR HOUSE

Interior decorating has become a specialized profession that requires years of training. There are many theories as to what the decorating process means to various people. One theory is that the way a woman decorates her house shows some of the inner secrets of her psyche. Her choice of furnishings, the pictures hanging on her walls, the type of furniture she prefers, and the way she arranges it all may be an elaborate Rorschach test that reveals her personality.

A woman psychologist has written a book entitled *Psycho Decorating,* in which she states that lamps, tables, chairs, and other furnishings indicate their owner's personality. Having surveyed eighty women, she claims women who prefer furniture with curved legs are inclined to be modest, responsible, obliging people who usually do what is expected of them. Women who choose furniture with straight legs rate high in achievement, doing their best in tasks requiring skill and effort. This writer also claims fabric textures show some aspects of personality. Use of velvet and corduroy indicates high exhibitionist needs, a highly developed conscience, and feelings about social justice.[2]

One possible translation of Proverbs 31:22 indicates superwife had carpets that were shaggy on both sides and pillows and bed coverlets. She worked at making these items, and her use of pillows may have anticipated modern decorators' use of toss pillows. Whether superwife's use of carpets and pillows would categorize her as the aggressive woman mentioned in *Psycho Decorating,* she certainly could not keep up with her modern sister, who is said to choose a glass-topped table to reflect her ambitious tendencies. If superwife had any type of mirror, it was probably polished brass and did not reflect anything very clearly.

Jesus told a story about a man who went to a wedding banquet held by a wealthy man. As was the custom, the host had provided an enormous wardrobe of garments for his guests to wear at the event. One guest did not bother to don a wedding garment. When the host discovered this man in his everyday clothing, he immediately ordered him ejected. Bible scholars have debated the correct interpretation of this story. Some claim it is that all our righteousness is as filthy rags and only faith in Christ can bring the cleansing we need. The second interpretation is that the garment represents the way we come across to others, our holiness without which no man can see God.

In either case, superwife is safe. She has that special faith, that reverential trust, and has given herself to a life of service to God and her fellow man, both of which may be symbolized by the way she dresses herself and her home.

CHAPTER 14

Being the Husband of a Successful Wife

 ot threatened by his wife's skills; her husband sits amongst the leaders at the city gate.

Prov. 31:23

NUN

In the course of gathering material for this book, I interviewed an outstanding Christian woman. As I warmed to my subject and discussed the desirable characteristics of an ideal woman, I sensed a less than enthusiastic response. Then she verbalized her apprehensions, "I guess we can use another book about women, particularly in the light of the lack of balance in many of our more recent books. But isn't it time something was written about men and their responsibilities within the family?" I could not agree more.

It is appropriate that in the midst of a highly flattering passage extolling the virtues of an unusual woman we are abruptly introduced to her husband, and he reappears periodically throughout the chapter. Although this passage is primarily concerned with the ideal woman, there is a secondary theme of the "ideal husband." The Bible has laid down a series of obligations for husbands, and a number of these are either directly or obliquely referred to in the thirty-first chapter of Proverbs.

Most of the translations follow the lead of the King James version: "Her husband is known in the gates" (Prov. 31:33). They place superwife's husband's professional activity at the city gate. The gate used to be important to the city as a protection against marauders. The city was surrounded by a wall and all who entered or left passed through the gate. It was the place of commerce, where merchants displayed their goods; of counseling by wise men; and of assembly by the elders chosen to sit on the council. Among these sat superwife's husband, "Her husband is well known, for he sits in the council chambers with the other civic leaders" (Prov. 31:23, LB). People who passed could see him in his place of honor.

Much of what superwife accomplished was due to the home from which she operated. Her husband provided her with a home and the financial support that enabled her to move out into her varied activities. In that earlier, more primitive, society, it was anticipated that for a woman to complete a pregnancy, give birth to a child, and rear it, she must have a husband who would stand by and care for her. Although the situation has changed today, a family unit without a responsible father will still have more difficulty coping with the strains of family living.

Many tests have been devised for measuring faith; and some of these have been very elaborate, as is seen in the historic creeds of the church. One test of orthodoxy or heresy depended on one single letter in a Greek word. The Bible suggests a far simpler test of faith, "But anyone who won't care for . . . those living in his own family has no right to say he is a Christian. Such a person is worse than a heathen" (1 Tim. 5:8, LB). The simple test of faith is that a man who does not care for his children has denied the faith.

In 1976, in Washington, D.C., there were more illegitimate than legitimate births, which meant that in most of these instances the man who had impregnated the woman refused to accept responsibility for his child. It requires little imagination to envisage the chaos that would result in a society where any great number of fathers were so irresponsible.

William Carey, the pioneer missionary who worked in India for so many years, was a lover of the scriptures. He translated either the Bible or portions of it into thirty-four languages. The Bible's message of the sanctity of the commitment to a wife held him faithful to his own marriage vow. Mrs. Carey had reluctantly left England after her husband's friend pleaded that their family be reunited. In 1785, Mrs. Carey fell ill with a severe case of dysentery and at the same time "morbid fantasies and tormenting fears took possession of her. . . . She grew the opposite of all she naturally was. Those whom she most tenderly loved she turned against. Her spirit passed into permanent gloom." For twelve years, Carey, a busy man laboring as a missionary, language teacher, horticulturist, and translator, refused to commit Mrs. Carey to an institution. He tended her needs with his own hands.[1]

Carey demonstrated the biblical principle of the husband and father of the house being a responsible individual. In a hedonistic age, when many men think only of their own selfish pleasures and have no sense of responsibility, we may need a return to the spirit of commitment to a wife and family demonstrated by Carey and the husband of superwife.

The book of Proverbs has an overriding concern for home and family life, and this concern is clearly demonstrated in the attitude of the father toward his children. The first nine chapters of Proverbs, nearly a quarter of the total book, is given over to a father's exhortation to his son. The recurring note of salutation is "To my son."

Melville's novel *Moby Dick* tells the story of a ship at sea under the command of the infamous Captain Ahab. This strange man spends his day in his cabin, brooding over the fate that left him with a wooden leg, which makes an ominous sound as he walks the deck of his ship. In his black depression, he lives for the day he will take his vengeance on the whale he thinks has caused all his misery. Spending long hours brooding over his misfortunes, he creates a horrible sense of impending doom over the entire ship.

Like Captain Ahab, a husband can set the mood for a home. The picture of this husband in Proverbs 31 shows him as involved with both his wife and his children in creating a good domestic atmosphere: "Her children stand up and bless her, so does her husband." He knows his children follow his example, so he stresses respect for their mother.

Against the background of masculine superiority so often found in the Old Testament, the Bible frequently introduces an important note as the husband is warned about the effects of his attitudes on his family. With regard to his children, he is told, "Fathers don't scold your children so much that they become discouraged and quit trying" (Col. 3:21). But it is particularly his wife who is to be his concern: "And you husbands must be loving and kind to your wives and not be bitter towards them or harsh" (Col. 3:19).

Yeats Brown, who thrilled untold numbers of readers with his book *The Lives of a Bengal Lancer,* used to tell the story of Yakbu Khan and the sniper. Trying to reopen the roads in the Khyber Pass, the workers for the British were constantly harassed by a lone sniper who, with deadly accuracy, kept picking off laborers and soldiers and leaving two or three men dead each day. After three months of this, with British troops fruitlessly searching for the sharpshooter, the British offered a thousand-rupee reward for anyone who could bring in the sniper dead or alive.

A boy named Yakbu Khan volunteered for the task. The veteran soldiers and workmen smiled at the idea of a kid with fuzzy cheeks fulfilling such a difficult mission; but because he asked only for a day off and the use of a rifle, his superiors granted his request. Later that day came the crack of a single rifle shot and news reached the camp that that sniper had been killed. As the boy confidently returned to the valley to collect his reward, the soldiers gathered around to ask him how he had found the sniper when the crack sharpshooters of the British Army had failed. Looking up for a moment from counting his newly acquired wealth, he said, "It was no trouble. I knew all his little tricks and hiding places. He was my father."[2]

A father should occupy a pivotal place in his family. He provides a model for his son, who sees what a man should be like; and for his daughter he represents the outside world and presents an image of the lover-husband with whom she will one day share her life. He is a partner to his wife as they build the type of family within which the best values can be developed.

DRAWING SPIRITUAL DIVIDENDS

The poem of wifely excellence tells about the relationship of this woman and her husband: "Her husband can trust her and she will richly satisfy his needs" (Prov. 31:11). Their relationship provides an opportunity for both giving and receiving. He trusts her and she supplies his needs.

The partnership of this husband and wife may have brought some unexpected benefits to him. We know there were material blessings as we read about the many enterprises in which his wife was involved, but the larger benefits of a husband-wife relationship become clearer in the New Testament writing of Peter. Peter's wife is probably the most prominent of all the disciples' spouses, being mentioned on at least two occasions in the Scripture. It is appropriate that Peter should be the one to remind husbands, "Remember you and your wife are partners in receiving God's blessings, and if you don't treat her as you should, your prayers will not get ready answers" (1 Pet. 3:7).

In devotional literature, the seeker after a deeper spiritual life is often urged to make greater efforts to jettison the sins that beset one by spending more time praying, reading the Bible more diligently, and attending worship. To these we might add, "Have a right relationship with your wife."

A SPIRITUAL LEADER

Remarking on the role of a husband in ancient Israel, the Bible encyclopedia notes, "The house father, by virtue of being the family head was the priest of the household."[3] This passage, with its teaching about what was pleasing to God, comes from the pen of King Lemuel, who is functioning as the leader of his family, ultimately becoming an example for the whole nation. Earlier in the book of Proverbs the spiritual responsibility of the father is noted: "The father of godly man has cause of joy" (Prov. 23:24). The father in his spiritual leadership rejoices when he sees he has been successful in leading his son to the pathway of service for God.

Right through the Bible the husband is the spiritual leader. At the Passover supper there comes a dramatic moment, when the child asks the question, "What does this mean? What is this ceremony about?" (Exod. 12:26, LB). The father replies by telling how God delivered his people from their captors in Egypt.

The charter of family life is set forth in Deuteronomy 6:4–7:

Hear, O Israel: The Lord our God is one Lord: And thou shalt love the Lord thy God with all thy heart, and with all thy soul, and with all thy might. And these words, which I command thee this day, shall be in thine heart: And thou shalt teach them diligently unto thy children, and shalt talk of them when thou sittest in thine house, and when thou walkest by the way, and when thou liest down, and when thou risest up.

Here is the heart of the faith, "The Lord our God is one Lord," and the response humans must make, "thou shalt love thy Lord thy God with all thine heart, with all thy soul, and with all thy might." Then follows very specific instructions as to how these truths are to be passed on to successive generations: "thou shalt talk of them when thou sittest in thine house, and when thou walkest by the way, when thou liest down, and when thou risest up."

A great emphasis is laid on the responsibility of the parents within the family, particularly the father. In verse 20 the son asks his father, "What mean the testimonies, and the statutes, and the judgments, which the Lord our God hath commanded you?" Put this into a modern setting and imagine a father reading the paper or watching his favorite television show. His son approaches and asks, "What mean the testimonies, and the statutes, and the judgments, which the Lord our God hath commanded you?" The father looks up, startled, and says, "What on earth are you talking about?" The son repeats the question, and the father says, "Goodness only knows, why come and worry me? Go ask the preacher or your Sunday school teacher!"

Modern parents have become adept at the art of delegating. We send our children to school for education, to the library for books, to the part for recreation, to the movies for entertainment, and to the church for religion. But there are some responsibilities that cannot be delegated. These belong fairly and squarely upon the parents' shoulders. The teaching of religion is one such responsibility.

Religion is *caught* as well as *taught.* An outstanding American preacher tells how much he hated math in high school and how he determined that when he went to college he would avoid every math course at any cost. At college he met a faculty member to whom he was attracted; and as their friendship grew, to his horror he discovered that his older friend was the math professor. His whole attitude toward math changed and he finally ended up taking every math course available. Within the family circle, the interpersonal relationships with parents will do more to teach religion than any amount of formal study.

This same note is found in an earlier chapter of Proverbs, where Solomon speaks about his relationship with his father and says, "I was the companion of my father" (Prov. 4:3).

LOVER—HUSBAND

Considering the Hebrew idea of the dominant male one might be surprised to note in the book of Proverbs that husband and wife are so frequently mentioned as being partners: "Listen to your father and mother" (Prov. 7:8, LB); "Loved, by my mother . . . and the companion of my father" (Prov. 4:3); "Young man obey your father and mother" (Prov. 6:20); "A rebellious son is a grief to his father and a bitter blow to his mother" (Prov. 17:25). It is clear this husband and wife must have had a good, open relationship; and this was probably due in large measure to the husband's willingness to talk.

A volume of readings on marriage and family that changes its contents from year to year has continually reprinted one paper, written in 1970. The constant repetition seems to indicate that the subject remains relevant. The title is "The Inexpressive American Male: A Tragedy of American Society." Its authors, two men, claim that in rearing our children we have been teaching them the traits of masculinity and feminity. Masculinity is associated with toughness, competitiveness, and aggressiveness, which is in contrast with the idea of feminity, expressed through gentleness, expressiveness, and responsiveness. A boy is taught from his earliest days, "You're a big boy and big boys don't cry." Parents proudly say of their son, "He's all boy," implying his aggressiveness, troublesomeness, and untidyness are typically masculine. He must not display any "sissy emotions."

The writers claim there are two ideals held up to growing boys. One is the cowboy type, a two-fisted, strong, silent male who does not show any tenderness or affection toward girls. His major concern may be his horse or, to bring it up to date, his car or his motorcycle. A second ideal is the playboy type, who apparently feels nothing, not even for his horse. He is typically nonfeeling and the woman in his life is a mere accessory. When he has a successful "love affair," it means he has been able to manipulate a woman and take her to bed, walking off to leave her as soon as his purpose has been served. So the writers of this paper conclude, "The inexpressive American male as a single man comes in two types: the inexpressive feeling man (the cowboy) and the inexpressive non-feeling man (the playboy)."[4] Whether he feels or not he does not let on.

When the inexpressive American male marries, he may face difficulties in his relationship with his wife. The situation is more difficult today than it used to be. In former days, the roles of husband and wife were more clearly defined and were task oriented. The man labored on the farm and protected his family. The woman specialized in the household tasks as a homemaker and mother of their children. But the situation is changing today; and as the task functions of marriage have declined, companionship and affection have emerged as important components of a marriage relationship. As one authority states it, "Companionship has emerged as the most valued aspect of marriage today." There can be no companionship without verbal communication.

Consider this scenario: The meal concluded, the husband buries his head in the evening paper. His wife is working at the last phases of cleaning up the remains of supper.

HER: Did you think it was a tasty meal?
HIM: Mm.
HER: Did you like the way I charcoaled the steak to a turn?
HIM: Mm.
HER: Do you think I manage the family budget well to be able to prepare such a well-balanced meal?
HIM: Mm.
HER: Do you like the way I made the centerpiece so economically with dried flowers?
HIM: Mm.
HER: Did the candles make you feel so romantic?
HIM: Mm.
HER: Oh, honey, you say the nicest things!

It may be a bit overplayed, but many women begin to get the idea that the only way to start a conversation with their husband is to pretend to be a novelist working on a piece of dialogue.

Of course, this problem is certainly not confined to Americans. King George V and his wife, Queen Mary, were two of the most beloved members of royalty ever to sit on the British throne. Their biographer says they had a family of six and were tremendously proud of them, but the children were "strangers to them emotionally." This attitude may have stemmed from the couple's relationship to each other. They occupied separate bedrooms and scarcely ever ate together alone. On one occasion King George sat down and wrote a letter to Queen Mary and thanked her for all the love and happiness she gave him. The queen replied, "What a pity it is you cannot *tell me* what you write, for I should appreciate it enormously."

Maybe we did not go back far enough when we began looking back at men and their function within the family. Instead of turning the clock back a mere one hundred years, perhaps we should have turned it back two or three thousand years to the time of the book of Proverbs. Notice the way this husband speaks about *his* wife: "There are many fine women in the world but you are the best of them all" (Prov. 31:29). Just imagine what that must have done for a wife. And in an interesting anticipation of the assertion that in a modern marriage a man sees his wife as his friend, the word used in an earlier chapter of Proverbs (Prov. 2:17) about a broken marriage uses a Hebrew word that literally means a sin against an old comrade. The wife was viewed as a friend and a comrade of the husband.

At least one of the secrets of the superwife in Proverbs 31 is the attitude of her husband. This man was not only a successful politician in his own right, a position he may have gained by his ability to work with people, but he played a significant role in making his wife what she became by his extraordinary powers of communication.

CHAPTER 15

Purple Collar Power

perating a business, she sews beautiful belted garmets, which she
sells to Phoenecian traders.

Prov. 31:24

SAMECH

President John Kennedy once remarked that in his leadership
of Great Britain, Winston Churchill brought a wonderful ally: He
mobilized the English language. Among Winston Churchill's stirring
speeches, in which he commended soldiers, sailors, and airmen, there
is an address delivered to six thousand women gathered in the Royal
Albert Hall in London. As he addressed them, Churchill acknowledged
their contributions and said Britain's war effort would not have been
possible if the women had not marched forward in millions to take up
the task and relieve men for service and combat units. Churchill speculated about the irony of the situation. It would seem women would have
made their greatest progress toward equality in times of peace. Then
in a characteristic turn of phrase he noted, "War is the teacher, a hard,
stern, efficient teacher."[1] Yet why should we wait for war?

From a wartime beginning during World War II, when Rosie the
riveter showed herself capable of the same work as men, women have
gradually emerged with new ideas of self-fulfillment. They have decided they have a right to earn money and can make a special contribution to the labor force. Many discussions of work use the collar as a
symbol. So we have "white collar" for clerical workers, "blue collar"
for manual laborers, and the recent "pink collar" for women in the

work force. Superwife was in many ways a businesswoman; but because we know she wore purple clothes, we will use the term "purple collar" to refer to her work.

THE WORKING WIFE

It is easier for a modern woman to get a job than it was for her grandmother. Many women still complain about the women's employment ghetto: waitresses, seamstresses, secretaries, bookkeepers, nurses, and teachers. One disgruntled woman complained, "I feel as if I have a typewriter chained around my neck." Nevertheless, new opportunities are opening so that a wife and mother can go to work. Patti Stahl worked as a receptionist at a doctor's office; and although she enjoyed the work, she often wished she could devote longer periods of time to her family. When Patti went on vacation, Ruby Balch filled in for her. Ruby told Patti how much she had enjoyed the work for "just three weeks." As the two women talked, an idea emerged. They could share the job. So they arranged to work alternative three-month periods. If Patti was working and became ill, Ruby took over. The two women love the arrangement, and the doctor who employs them agrees it is a success.

When Clifford Teague heard his secretary, Virginia Ellis, was leaving, he had a sinking feeling. He had done everything he could to keep her, including giving her a salary raise and permission to leave early in the afternoons to get home to her children. Then Clifford had an idea. If Virginia needed so badly to be with her children, maybe part-time help would be the answer. He advertised a part-time position and in his words, "Those women came out of the woodwork, college degreed highly trained mothers of children who wanted to work just a portion of the day." Many women do not wish to work a full week but would be glad to work a limited number of hours.

Many wives used to consider school teaching the ideal profession because they could leave in the morning with their school-age children and be home again when they returned. The introduction of "flex-itime" which enables workers to set their own hours, has opened up many opportunities for wives and mothers with children in school.

When Nora Wiley took an office job, she looked around for someone to take care of her two preschool children during the day. The
arrangements worked out just fine. One afternoon she arrived home
early from work and told the sitter she could leave right away if she
wished. The sitter smiled, "There's no need for that. I need to hang
around until it is time for me to pick up my children from their sitter."

The sitter who employs a sitter while she works for the office worker
demonstrates the different levels of profitability. The elderly woman
who works as a sitter for a sitter may not make much money, but she
has emotional and psychological rewards. And the woman who looks
after another woman's children while leaving her own with a sitter has
at least a change of locale and a small financial gain.

Because 46 percent of American women work outside the home,
either full- or part-time, more and more wives are considering the
option of contributing to family income. Before deciding to do so,
however, they should count the costs. There are pros and cons to the
working wife situation that every would-be working wife should consider. The following are some advantages a working wife can enjoy:

1. She can gain a sense of personal satisfaction and achievement.
   Doing something in her own right, she may develop a set of
   interests apart from her husband and family.
2. She may enable the family to enjoy a higher standard of living,
   although this might be less than it appears to be, as we shall see
   later.
3. She will gain certain fringe benefits: discounts, vacation pay,
   group insurance, pension plans, and so forth. She can also qualify
   for social security in her own right, providing support for her
   family if she dies while the children are under eighteen.
4. Children *may* develop more self-reliance and take more initiative
   as they accept more home responsibilities. The working mother
   is less likely to "smother love" her offspring.
5. There is a certain therapeutic value. An employed woman may
   think less of her troubles, both real and imagined, when she has
   other responsibilities.
6. She may gain valuable experience that will aid her if she has to

go to work later in life should her husband die or become disabled.

7. She will have an appreciation for and understanding of working conditions and indirectly, a keener insight into her husband's problems at his job and the difficulties that beset her children.

8. The home *may* become more of a cooperative venture, with the husband taking an active role in the housekeeping and the children assuming responsibilities earlier. Not the word "may."

9. She may show more interest in her appearance and thus develop into a more attractive person, which no husband should resent.

But lest we get carried away with all this, we should note there are some debits in this balance. The working mother may labor under a number of disadvantages, including the following:

1. Employed mothers may find their children suffer emotionally and otherwise when left in the care of other people. Very small children may be particularly vulnerable. All the kids who return home from school to an empty house may constitute an adjustment problem. The question in most mother's minds is what will happen to the children, and this is one that should be carefully considered.

2. Working mothers may find they do not earn nearly as much money as they imagined they would. Taxes and job-related expenses eat up a third to a half of the average woman's paycheck. She will pay income taxes, social security, and the added income may throw her husband into a higher tax bracket. Then add union dues, transportation, uniforms, extra clothes, beauty aides, household helps, and so forth. On the average, the working mother who must employ household help for her children is fortunate to break even. With no small children, her net earnings will be as little as one-half of her gross income.

3. Her husband may resent her employment. He may consider it a blow to his pride, and they may have disagreements as to how the wife's income is to be spent.

4. If the family increases its standard of living on the basis of her income, there will be difficult adjustments if she has to quit work because of illness or pregnancy.

5. The working wife may be so exhausted physically and emotionally that she neglects her role as a wife. When she comes home tired from work, she may not feel like fulfilling her role as wife.
6. There is a good chance there is going to be some problem about the division of labor within the home. There are many husbands who are not very good when it comes to housework.

So think before making this all-important decision. Do not forget to count the costs. Sit down and realistically work out all the expenses; ask yourself if it is really worthwhile.

SHARE THE WORK AND SPREAD THE LEISURE

A wife's decision to take a job outside the home is just the beginning of a whole group of problems she will have to face, not the least of which is how to manage a new position as well as carry on her domestic responsibilities. One working wife claimed she was a modern Cinderella. Like that famous female who was the belle of the ball until the clock struck twelve, she was a professional woman during working hours, accepted by collegues and commended for her superior skills. But the moment the clock struck, not twelve but five, she was plunged into domestic responsibilities and, if not the servant of ugly sisters, at least a guide and mentor of a husband and a family who had always considered her to be at their beck and call.

Successful working wives learn to set priorities and enlist the aid of family members. Many a wife is driven by a compulsion to make sure the house is antiseptically clean and have the motto, "A place for everything and everything in its place." But when this woman goes to work, some things will change. One teenager had a poster on her wall, "Caution: human beings here, handle with care." People rather than things must be the working mother's priority.

To succeed as a working mother, a wife must enlist the aid of all the family members. No longer can the family afford the luxury of designating some chores as men's work and some as women's work. They must designate household chores as work, just work, neither male nor female. Sometimes children can trade chores if it makes them happier, but each child must accept some responsibility.

Husbands are particularly guilty of stereotyping male and female roles. As a concession to this, one wife, noticing hubby's hangdog look as he scraped the dishes, suggested, "Honey, you men have a special way with mechanical things. Let me scrape the dishes while you handle the vacuum cleaner this morning." She was rewarded the following Saturday when her husband wheeled the vacuum past her with the comment, "What's the big deal with housework? It just needs a little organization."

One woman concluded that being a successful working mother required the organizational skill of a corporation president, the energy of the bionic woman, the humor of a circus clown, and above everything else a family with two mottoes: "Share the work and spread the leisure" and "The family that works together and plays together stays together." Or she may need some of the skills of superwife.

My early years as a wife and mother coincided with my entry into the life of a minister's wife. In those days churches would not stand for a preacher's spouse working. Oh, they wanted her to work alright, but not outside the church. If she had time left over from her domestic chores, it was expected she would turn her energies toward church life. Later when John was employed by the convention, I spent long hours working alongside him in a bookstore, which was an important part of the convention's enterprise. I had flexible hours and enjoyed working among books and meeting so many people. An unexpected bonus came from my son. Immediately after school let out each afternoon, he would come to the bookstore and go home with us. Always interested in books, he became an omnivorous reader as he waited for us to close the store. I believe his reading habits, formed in part in that bookstore, prepared him for his outstanding career in adult life.

My experience in the bookstore paid off in an unexpected way in later years. John became a prolific writer, twenty-five books at last count. Because many of these had to do with home and family life, I had a growing conviction that families need literature. So I set up Family Enrichment Supply, which makes John's books available at our numerous conferences and speaking engagements.

When my husband left our native Australia for the United States,

I became responsible for the family and went to work full-time in the bookstore. I soon discovered that working all day at set hours was quite a change from a part-time position where I chose my own hours, and I struggled with the problem of caring for my preschool son. Fortunately, his grandmother loved looking after him, always calling him "my little angel." But by the time she was through spoiling him, he was more devil than angel.

I would suggest a wife contemplating employment consider the following factors:

1. *Salary. How much can you expect to earn in a year?*
2. *Taxes. How much will be deducted annually from your paycheck for federal, state, and local taxes and for social security? How much in additional taxes will your husband have to pay because of the increase in your family income?*
3. *Company deductions. How much will you have to contribute toward medical insurance, pension plan, and so forth?*
4. *Dues. If union membership is required, what will it cost to join? What are the dues?*
5. *Transportation. What will it cost to commute to and from the job? If you use your own car, allow for gas, oil, repairs, maintenance, and additional insurance premium you may have to pay when the car is used to commute.*
6. *Lunches. How much will it cost to eat out, allowing for an occasional splurge?*
7. *Clothing. How much can you realistically expect to spend for additional clothing needed for the job? How much for extra dry cleaning and shoe repairs?*
8. *Child care. If you have small children, what will it cost to provide care in a day care center or by a sitter at home?*

By simply adding up these and any other expenses that might be necessary in your particular case and subtracting the annual total from your potential salary, you will be able to determine the amount you will actually gain from working outside the home.

CHAPTER 16

Laughing at the Future

alpably strong and dignified, she laughs at the future.
Prov. 31:25

A Y I N

Lowell Thomas, veteran filmmaker, author, and broadcaster, was entranced with the World War I exploits of Count Felix von Luckner, who from his native Germany had sneaked through the British blockade in the North Sea in his specially equipped raider-sailing ship *Seedler* (*Sea Eagle*). The count cruised the sea lanes of the world, wreaking havoc and destruction on Allied shipping, destroying valuable craft with gunfire, but always taking great pains to see no harm befell the sailors. As he apprehended each new craft, its crew and provisions were transferred to the *Seedler,* where the astonished detainees were ushered into a life of fun and frolic more like a holiday cruise than a war patrol. Von Luckner later boasted, "No one, no mother, wife, child or father ever had to shed a single tear because of any harm we brought to a loved one." Full of fun and wit, this giant of a man romped through life and once told his biographer, "We all came into the world crying while everyone else was laughing. By Joe, I mean to go out laughing— let others do the crying."[1] Von Luckner was laughing at the future.

For many women the future is no laughing matter. Although women are sometimes referred to as the "weaker sex" and may not be able to bring forth the short bursts of brute strength of the male, when it comes to staying power, they leave men standing still. When counseling a couple preparing for marriage, I half seriously tell the bride-to-be, "Make sure he has a good insurance policy on his life, for there is a good chance you will outlive him by ten years." If you doubt my advice, look over any group of elderly people. You will see the ever-diminishing number of males with the passing of years. Despite their greater longevity, or perhaps because of it, many women are apprehensive about the latter years of life.

OLD-AGE ASSISTANCE

In many of the primitive societies of the world, families are dominated by the aged matriarch, who is respected and even feared by the younger members of the family. This is not so in modern Western society. England's desperate hours in World War II caused her to send young men into the skies in their Spitfires and Hurricanes to perform the deeds of which Winston Churchill said, "Never in the field of human endeavor have so many owed so much to so few."[2] Among the few was a young man who before he left on a mission sat down and wrote a letter to his mother. He failed to return and was listed as missing, probably dead. The youthful pilot in his last communication with his mother reaffirmed his belief in the cause for which he fought, thanked her for all she had done for him, and concluded, *"Thus at my early age my earthly mission is already fulfilled and I am prepared to die with just one regret—that I could not devote myself to making your declining years more happy by being with you."* The statement is unusual enough to attract attention in a day when the most pressing thought of youth seems to be, "How can I get away from my family responsibilities?" And most of the sentiment today is in favor of the government taking over the responsibility for the aging members of the population.

The young airman's philosophy seems closely related to the wisdom of the East. A reporter for Hong Kong radio once asked me what I thought of the Chinese family. I recounted how we had entertained a Chinese student in the United States; and when we arrived in Hong Kong, there was our student's family waiting to welcome us. There stood a large group of people—brothers, sisters, uncles, aunts, grandparents, and sundry other relatives—waiting to welcome and present us with an invitation to a special meal. I was tremendously impressed by the solidarity of the extended Chinese family as manifested by this group. The reporter chuckled, "Oh that's because we don't have social security. A mother needs a large, tightly knit family to look after her in her old age." It is also the idea of the book of Proverbs, which gives responsibility for older parents to the children and warns them, "A son who mistreats his father and mother is a public disgrace" (Prov. 19:26, LB). Many of the plans of the welfare state fail to equal the quality of family care for the elderly, and the price tag soars to incredible heights.

What a surprise she would have been in for if superwife had lived today and seen how we Westerners treat our older citizens. There is a good chance she would have joined the Gray Panthers, a highly vocal movement led by seventy-two-year-old Maggie Kuhn, who was forced to retire from her job with the Presbyterian church missions at age sixty-five and thus became vividly aware of ageism. She says we treat old people as "wrinkled babies" and put them in nursing homes and homes for the elderly, which are little more than "glorified play pens."

With relentless logic, Kuhn points out that the Masai in Kenya or the Chinese revere old people, but in the United States we are caught up with the throwaway syndrome and scrap our old people like worn-out hulks. She and her organization are out to destroy what she calls the rotten myths about old age: "You know, all of use are supposed to be alike: crotchety and cranky, our brains shriveling up, and our sex organs withering away. That, of course, is nonsense. Many of us are livelier and smarter than ever. And as for sex, I'm afraid it's our adult children who are the prudes and who pass on myths about 'dirty old men' and 'dirty old ladies.' "[3]

What is Maggie's answer? First, abolish compulsory retirement. Second, encourage what she calls "intergenerational living," with older and younger people living together. She laments, "Today, young people scarcely get to see an old person up close—that is, until they become one."[4] This, of course, is just what the Bible teaches about the generations living together in a family that is responsible for the welfare of all its members, young and old. Blessed is the woman who has a large family that is concerned about her. In a very real sense she is able to "laugh at the future."

FACTORS IN HEALTH

The web of relationships within a family not only provides adequate physical care for an aging woman, but it may be an important factor in her state of health and well-being. A researcher has developed the rather startling idea that an individual's health is closely related to the types of interpersonal relationships in which she is involved. A study made in Utah and Nevada dramatized the role of networks of relationships. Both states have adult education rates that are among the highest in the nation and almost identical; the average per-capita income in Utah lags behind Nevada by about $1000 a year; and the number of people living in urban areas in the two states is almost the same. The major differences between the two states is in the life-styles of their populations. Nevada has established a record as a divorce capital, has a highly mobile population, and has made gambling a basic industry. Utah's large Mormon population of nondrinkers and nonsmokers maintains stable lives, secure marriages, and strong family units. Victor Fuchs in *Who Shall Live* notes, "More than twenty percent of Nevada's males aged 35–64 are single, widowed, divorced or not living with their spouses. Of those who are married with spouse present, more than one-third had been previously widowed or divorced. In Utah, comparable figures are half as large."[5]

A federal government map indicating death rates from cardiovascular diseases shows Nevada has the unenviable record of being number one in the way it shortens white people's lives. The same high rate is true of almost every other cause of death. Utah has one of the lowest death rates in the nation. What factors cause the difference between the two states? Is it air, water, education, topography, or wealth? The greatest difference appears to be Utah's stable population, with its emphasis on the strength of religious and family relationships.

Acknowledging the factors generally charged with destroying health, such as obesity, diet, lack of exercise, and smoking, one writer has come up with the startling premise that one very obvious consideration may have been overlooked and "A person's life may be shortened by lack of human companionship."[6] He presents some evidence to back up his assertion, including statistics indicating death rate from heart disease is two to five times higher among nonmarried individuals and in almost every type of cancer, a disease unambiguously physical in nature, married people have lower mortality rates than the unmarried. He states, "U.S. mortality rates for all causes of death . . . are consistently higher for divorced, single and widowed individuals of both sexes and all races. Some of the increased death rates in unmarried individuals are astounding, rising as high as ten times the rates for married individuals of comparable ages."[7] So appears an entirely new factor in the speculation as to why some people live longer than others: Marital status is one of the best predictors of health, disease, and death.

Superwife, who laughs at the future, had a very real basis for her confidence. She had a capable and appreciative husband and a group of children who constantly acknowledged all her family endeavors. Giving herself for her family, she discovered her family in turn brought an extra dimension to her life and paved the way for long and fruitful years.

The startling indication of the part relationships play in physical health should not sidetrack us from the physical components of a healthy body. It would be the height of stupidity for a woman to live on fatty foods; to loll around all day without exercising, smoking, imbibing alcohol, allowing herself to grow increasingly obese; and to take refuge in the fact that she has a devoted family who cares and a husband who loves her.

There are several ways to refer to the body of a deceased human. The medically minded call it a "cadaver," which sounds rather like a reference to some nonhuman species. An undertaker I knew sometimes startled people by asking what they wanted done with "the remains," a term suggestive of the leftovers from a meal that might be kept in the refrigerator. The vague reference to "the departed" contains at least an inference that he might just be out for lunch. "Corpse" has a certain ominous note. I think the most graphic, accurate, and descriptive word is the colloquialism "stiff." It sums up the essential difference between life and death. Life means movement; complete lack of movement, as indicated by the word "stiff," graphically describes death. Movement is a sign of life; as Dr. Daniel J. Leithauser expresses it, "Absolute inactivity is death."[9]

Once we accept this basic concept, we must also accept the reverse. Movement or activity is the sign of life, and this may give us a clue to superwife's ability to laugh at the future. Just look at the description in Proverbs 31 of her life and all the activities she crowds into her busy days:

1. *Partner.* "She will not hinder him (her husband) but help him all her life" [v. 12].
2. *Weaver.* "She finds wool and flax and busily spins it" [v. 13].
3. *Importer.* "She buys imported goods, brought by ship from distant parts" [v. 14].
4. *Early riser.* "She gets up before dawn to prepare breakfast for her household" [v. 15].
5. *Manager.* "She plans the day's work for her servant girls" [v. 15].
6. *Realtor.* "She goes out to inspect a field and buys it" [v. 16].
7. *Horticulturalist.* "With her own hand she plants a vineyard" [v. 16].
8. *Shopper.* "She watches for bargains" [v. 18].
9. *Philanthropist.* "She sews for the poor and generously gives to the needy" [v. 19–20].
10. *Seamstress.* "She also upholsters with finest tapestry; her own clothing is beautifully made" [v. 22].
11. *Energetic.* "Is never lazy" [v. 27].

Just reading about superwife's wide variety of activities is enough to tire a lesser mortal.

Milly Cooper suddenly realized she could not join superwife in laughing at the future. It all started one night when she and her husband were watching television and he asked her to take his resting pulse. It was fifty beats a minute. Then he took hers and reported it at eighty beats a minute. He pointed out that while they slept that night his and her hearts would pump the same amount of blood but her heart would beat about ten thousand times more than his because she was not in condition. He added with an irritating masculine logic, "You're just going to wear out faster than I will." Milly sat and pondered the situation. Visions of her handsome, trim doctor husband as a widower and the target for husband-hunting widows, spinsters, and divorcees flitted through her head. She determined to do something about the situation and embarked on an exercise program. Milly had an advantage because her husband, Dr. Kenneth Cooper, is the founder of the aerobics system, which is probably the most successful scientifically based exercise program in existence today.

In one way Cooper is answering Ponce de León, who in 1513 landed on Florida's shore in search of the mythical fountain of youth, hopeful of finding a way to extend life. The trouble was that he was looking for the wrong substance. He did not need a liquid; he needed a gas— oxygen. If the general population only realized the importance of supplying oxygen to the body, the country would be faced with the biggest craze yet. Our need for oxygen is far more important than our need for food. We can survive without food up to one hundred and eighty days. We can go without water as long as five to seven days. But without oxygen our sensitive brain cells die after only six to eight minutes. The biggest single problem of life is getting a good supply of this all-important gas into the body.

Every movable part of the human body needs action. This action should lead to the "training effect," which comes from exercise producing more blood, more red blood cells, more hemoglobin, and more blood plasma. The result is a greater delivery capacity of oxygen and a much more rapid return and expulsion of wastes. Cooper concludes about the circulatory system, "Increase its work load and it increases its efficiency. Sit around and do nothing and it deteriorates. It's as simple as that."[9]

At the center of this intricate operation is a magnificent ten-and-one-half-ounce pump that sends the oxygenated blood from the lungs through the body. The condition of this remarkable instrument, the heart, is all-important. Dr. Cooper points out a anomaly, "Ironically, the heart works faster and less efficiently when you give it little to do than it does when you make more demands upon it. It is a remarkable engine."[10] The big problem we face in our sedentary society is that we make few demands on our heart and consequently it becomes flabby. The simplest answer is exercise, planned and vigorously carried out.

To be able to laugh at the future, you must work hard and regularly in the present. You cannot store fitness; you must work at it week by week. But all of this pays off. Describing the benefits of her aerobics program, Milly Cooper says her dress size went from twelve to eight, she lost ten pounds, her eating habits improved, she became less tense, she sleeps better, and she gained an enhanced self-image and an awareness of her husband's pride in her. All this and a longer life too! If you wish to laugh at the future, get into an exercise program. Take a look at the box at the end of this chapter. As Russ Harris says, "You don't stop exercising because you get old, you get old because you stop exercising."

While waiting in the check-in line at the Louisville, Kentucky, airport, I realized we were standing behind the best-known bearded American since Abraham Lincoln: Colonel Harlan Sanders, the originator of Kentucky fried chicken. There he stood in his white suit, goatee, walking stick, and black string tie, looking for all the world like he had just stepped off the chicken bucket.

Thrilled at the opportunity to visit with such a well-known personality, I suggested we go over and talk with him. My husband demurred, reminding me that every individual is entitled to his own private life without being stopped by every curious bystander. He put his foot down and insisted we leave the colonel alone.

Ten minutes later, as we were talking with our new friend, he produced his engagement schedule with obvious pride. In one month he had engagements for thirty of the thirty-one days. It certainly looked like what some people would call a punishing schedule. Queried about this, Sanders, his eyes twinkling, replied, "Wouldn't it be awful to wake up in the morning and have nothing to do?"

Colonel Sanders certainly has plenty to do. He lives on what he describes as a small farm outside of Louisville, rises at 4 A.M. to work "before the day gets too hot," and raises his own food organically. He lives on his social security check and his eye twinkles again as he adds,

"I save my salary for my old age." This eighty-seven-year-old man told me, "I have asked the Lord for thirteen more years. Then when I reach my century mark, I will give my time to working with senior citizens." Like our ideal wife, he is laughing at the future.

I have not quite gotten around to laughing at the future myself, and I suppose most women face the later years of life with something less than equanimity. When it comes to activity, I have always moved rapidly; a woman must when she has children and a workaholic husband. Then I discovered that routine movements do little for my circulatory system. My husband was sold on Dr. Cooper's aerobics program and had started a swimming regimen. Day after day I went and watched him. My bouffant hairstyle was my pride and joy. Every Friday I had an eight o'clock appointment at the beauty shop. If I swam, I would mess up my hair.

As I sat watching John so obviously enjoying his swimming while I posed on the edge of the pool dangling my feet in the water, something within me snapped. I went to the hairstylist and had my hair cut off. I suddenly had a new freedom, no more beauty shop appointments, a nice little saving in cash, and the joy of plunging and frolicking in the pool. Soon I set about seriously following the aerobic tables and working for my thirty points per week. I was particularly proud months later when I received my Red Cross patch for swimming fifty miles. I had always been a tennis nut; now I cycle and swim and work for my aerobic points. I am learning how to laugh at the future. Some authorities claim all the evidence is not in yet to show that exercise really prolongs life. If it does not, as I head for that land where "His servants love to serve Him," I will be able to say I had a great time making it as far as I did.

An enthusiastic Russian propagandist was hard at work trying to convince an Englishman of the superiority of the Marxist system over the English. Finally, in derision he said, "You English people are always talking about your history; you are slaves to the past." The Englishman reminded the Russian that in his system many of the desirable amenities of life were forfeited for the future and noted, "You Marxists are slaves to the future." Not so with superwife. She laughed at the future, largely because of a concerned family, close personal relationships, and an active life.

THE ACTIVITY CONCEPT

Do not overlook the possibilities in ordinary activities of life. One expert has suggested the shopping expedition can be an exercise experience, reaching down to lower shelves, twisting around for an item, carrying out the sacks of groceries.

Three good principles for incorporating activity into life:

1. Do not lie when you can sit.
2. Do not sit when you can stand.
3. Do not stand when you can move.

A good exercise program requires effort and at least twenty minutes a day. Exercise for four or five minutes a day will not accomplish very much.

Work up to it gradually. The Greeks had a myth about a man who picked up a calf and carried it. He continued daily; and as the calf grew, so did his strength.

Do it regularly. Studies show that unexercised muscles deteriorate rapidly. After three days of immobility, an individual loses as much as one-fifth of his maximum muscle strength. One study by NASA scientists showed daily exercise is desirable; but if this is not possible, exercise on three nonconsecutive days each week will maintain an adequate level.

Exercise sensibly. If your breathing has not returned to normal within five to ten minutes after exercising, there is a good chance you may be overdoing it.

Exercise need not dominate your life. Fit it into your life-style. I ride a stationary bike each morning while watching two courses on "Sunrise Semester." I accumulate my "points" and learn a lot at the same time.

Get a copy of *Aerobics* by Cooper. It is the work of an enthusiast and has information that will help you develop a good exercise program that will lead to physical fitness.

CHAPTER 17

The Delicate Art of Conversation

 uietly attentive, she makes a wise response, always speaking with kindness.

Prov. 31:26

PEH

According to the enemies of Chiang Ch'ing (Azure River), the most powerful man in the world in terms of the number of people who gave him their allegiance, whose words or sayings were revered, and who was virtually deified by his millions of followers, could not stand up to one talkative woman. Mao Tse-tung's strong-minded wife was at his side for many years, and when he died, her enemies feared she might try to seize power. They launched an attack on her, accusing Chiang Ch'ing of causing the death of their beloved Chairman Mao. A major accusation was that Chiang Ch'ing had nagged her husband to death.

The view of women as naggers is not new. In many societies where women were forced into an inferior role by the physically stronger males, they frequently turned to the only weapon they had—their tongue. So the book of Proverbs often portrays women in a somewhat less than flattering manner as far as their communications are concerned.

A beautiful woman lacking discretion . . . is like a fine gold ring in a pig's snout [Prov. 11:22, LB].

It is better to live in the corner of an attic than with a crabby woman in a lovely home [Prov. 21:9, LB].

Better to live in the desert than with a quarrelsome, complaining woman [Prov. 21:19, LB].

A constant dripping on a rainy day and a cranky woman are much alike! You can no more stop her complaints than you can stop the wind or hold onto anything with oil-slick hands [Prov. 27:15–16, LB].

The overall impression is that the women of Solomon's day are only opening their mouths to quarrel, nag, complain, or make indiscrete statements. All of this is in vivid contrast of the ideal woman portrayed in the poem of wifely excellence. Verse 26 describes a woman who is an excellent communicator, pays attention, has something worthwhile to say, and expresses herself with great skill and finesse.

PAYING ATTENTION

"When she speaks"—the statement in the Living Bible implies the woman considers carefully before she utters a word. She pays attention and thinks over what has been said before she responds. She knows communication is a two-way process. One must learn to listen before speaking. If one has learned to pay attention and listen, one will be a better speaker.

I once attended a seminar conducted by an eminent sociologist. He was an authority and obviously knew his subject. At the conclusion of his presentation, he announced he had come to hear as well as to speak. He invited the group members to express their opinions and ask questions about the subject under discussion. This scientist's reactions to the people who spoke were a fascinating study in themselves. He stared at a somewhat verbose questioner as if trying to lull him into a hypnotic trance and silence. If a participant persisted, the sociologist's bushy eyebrows began a rhythmic movement like two gyrating caterpillars poking faces at one another. His rather large red lips shaped unspoken words, occasionally reinforced by strange, incoherent sounds. His ham-like hands reached out in mesmeric movements. When he spoke, he said, "Go on"; but every response of his body shouted, "Keep quiet and let me talk."

The ideal wife in Proverbs 31:26 illustrates what Solomon wrote about in his companion book of Ecclesiastes where he says there is a time for every activity. Among other things, he says there is a time to speak and a time to keep silent. Most of us agree there is a time to speak; we feel it would be a tragedy if there were not some voice upon the air, preferably our own. But Solomon says there is also a time to keep silent. About this we are not quite sure. A poet expresses the misgiving that often enters the heart of the listener.

> I bend a sympathetic ear
> To other people's woes,
> However dull it is to hear
> Their real or fancied throes.
> I pay to every gloomy line
> Attention undiminished,
> Because I plan to start on mine
> The moment theirs are finished.[1]

Unfortunately, this is the attitude of many of us. We are listening to fill in the time until we get the opportunity to speak.

A whole new generation of psychologists known as behavior shapers is instructing parents and teachers in the art of changing behavior. They teach that all behavior is carried on in terms of its consequences. When there are good consequences, behavior is repeated; when bad consequences ensue, behavior is diminished and ultimately terminated. This principle has led to a quest for rewards and punishments. Many studies show the greatest reward one human being can give another is attention and the greatest punishment is withdrawal of attention. As a housewife, you have to make many payments, rent, utilities, loan installments; but remember, if you are to be a good conversationalist, you must learn to pay the golden coin of attention.

ASKING QUESTIONS

Of superwife it is said, "Her words are wise" (Prov. 31:26). Some Bible scholars doubt that the King Lemuel mentioned in this passage was an individual. It may be a pseudonym used by King Solomon. This idea is widely held by Jewish commentators. If the assumption is correct, the writer of this passage knew a lot about talking with women. One celebrated conversation with the queen of Sheba has been carefully documented in the Bible. The queen of Sheba came to see Solomon so she could learn of his wisdom. They spent long hours together while the queen tested him by asking questions and "Solomon answered all her questions" (1 Kings 10:3). The queen was such a skillful questioner that she showed Solomon at his best.

Descendants of the queen of Sheba who want to be good conversationalists could easily learn some lessons from her, the most important of which might be to acquire listening skills. They should then acquire what one writer has called "the delicate art of asking questions."[2] The basic questioning technique to encourage conversation is never to ask a question that can be answered with "yes" or "no." Suppose you are talking with Jennifer Leach, who appears anxious and in need of someone to talk to. One way of approaching it would be to say, "Do you like living with your sister?" This approach will invite a response of "yes" or "no," and you will sit there looking at each other. A more profitable approach would be to say "How do you feel about living with your sister?" This may evoke a statement about her feelings and concerns.

A question can often get out of a difficult situation. A mother, worried about the hostility her daughter displayed when asked to be in by a certain hour, decided to try a different tactic. When the moment of confrontation came, Mrs. Harrison simply asked, "Well, Lisa, what time do you think you should be in?" To her amazement, Lisa responded, "I think eleven-thirty would be okay." Mrs. Harrison had found an at least partial answer to the problem.

Sarah Wilson was faced with a delicate situation when Jennifer Williams came to borrow her china for a special dinner she was giving for her husband's boss. Sarah had bragged about her dinner service, which had belonged to her grandmother, and in a weak moment had said to Jennifer, "You can use it one of these times." Now here was Jennifer and Sarah really did not want to lend it. Instead of coming straight out with a refusal she thought might offend, she asked a question, "Jennifer, how would you respond if you owned the china?

Remember it is a family treasure, very old and a little fragile. If I asked you to lend it to me, would you do it?" Jennifer thought for a moment, "I don't think I would lend it."

Learn the skill of the question and like the fabled queen of Sheba you may discover many things you did not know before and at the same time increase other people's appreciation of you.

When Mrs. Hansen found herself seated at the banquet alongside Mr. Edwin Black, she immediately sense a challenge. Mr. Black, sitting stiffly in his unaccustomed tuxedo, looked like a man just ushered into a torture chamber. He was obviously very ill at ease. Mrs. Hansen went to work on him.

Convinced of the power of the question, this astute woman queried her banquet partner concerning his view of the weather, the political scene, the city bond election, and his family. Despite all these efforts, her questions were greeted with monosyllabic replies. Mr. Black was not hostile—just hopeless in a situation like this—but he had enough native intelligence to realize what his dinner partner was trying to do.

Molly Hansen had reached the end of her tether. She had just about decided to lapse into silence and endure the ordeal when Mr. Black came up with a question to help her with her questions and spoke his first sentence, "Why not try pies?" Quick to pick up on a cue, Mrs. Hansen asked, "Will you please tell me something about pies?"

It turned out that Mr. Black, while working in a bakery, had stumbled upon a new way to make pies and patented a unique pie-making machine. From the process he had amassed a considerable fortune. Once started, he talked nonstop about materials, types, food values, and varieties of taste and provided Mrs. Hansen with some fascinating insights into an area about which she formerly knew nothing. Later, at a posh affair at the women's club, when conversation bogged down Mrs. Hansen asked a question that started a lively discussion, "Do you know how they fry pies?"

In one sense a good conversationalist is a group facilitator of the interaction taking place between two or more people involved in discussion. A competent conversationalist is exercising the same skills as the group therapist. Mrs. Hanson saw Mr. Black as an isolate, a man left out of the conversation. Suppose at the next social function she had seen him sitting over in a corner by himself and feeling miserable. Using a good group therapy technique, she would probably say, "Mr. Black, why don't you tell us something about that new device for making pies?"

Probably the biggest single problem in group therapy is the process known as "subgrouping." In subgrouping, a couple of participants, by talking to each other and ignoring the rest of the group, set up a little group of their own. It sometimes takes the form of people "whispering" to each other, perhaps behind a sheltering hand. Such subgrouping will sabotage any real effort at good conversation involving the whole group.

A good hostess attacks this problem head on. Depending on your knowledge of the group, you can approach it in several ways. You can come right out and say, "Come on, you two over there, you're subgrouping; let us in on what is happening." If you need a more tactful approach, you can say, "You two are having such an interesting time; we'd like to know what you're talking about."

Be on your guard for Mr. Black's opposite, the conversational hijacker. In any group of people there are always enthusiasts who are lying in wait for an opportunity to hijack a conversation. Jean Jones, for example, is an astrology enthusiast. Telling about her trip to Germany, Shirley Harris says, "We arrived in Garmisch on my birthday, the eleventh of May." Jean immediately takes over, "May eleventh, you must be a Taurus, I'll bet you. . . ." A good host or hostess stands ready for such an eventuality and holds off the would-be hijacker, "That's interesting, but of course we want to hear about Shirley's stay in Garmisch. Tell us about Garmisch, Shirley."

THE TRAFFIC LIGHTS

Carrying on a conversation resembles driving a car down a long road with a light at every cross street. The conversational green light is the day you hit it just right, and the lights changed with beautiful regularity to encourage you to move right on down the highway. These are the moments to cherish in conversation. You have the floor. All the members of the party are indicating their interest. The collective message of the group is "tell me more" or "right on."

Watch for amber. It is a warning. People cough, begin to look around the room, grow very restless, take surreptitious glances at their watches. Some people accelerate on an amber light and manage to get through. You might introduce a new element, touch some responsive chord, raise or lower your voice, and just get by. But if you take no action, you have had it.

SOME CONVERSATION STOPPERS

"I know I'm wasting my breath, but. . . ."

"No one in his right mind could believe that. . . ."

"Everybody knows that. . . ."

"Where did you get that goofy idea?"

"It really isn't any of my business but. . . ."

"Why do you always think you know more than anybody else?"

"If you're not interested in hearing the facts . . . okay."

"Whoever told you you could wear blue?"

"Well, sweetie, those pants don't do a thing for you."

"Are you trying to be funny?"

"I don't want to hurt your feelings but. . . ."

"If I tell you something, will you promise not to get mad?"

Amber also shows itself when your listeners begin to use "interrupt gestures." They take a variety of forms and may hark back to school days, when we raised our hands to indicate we wanted to speak. One raises one's hand four to six inches, then may touch one's ear lobe. Other varieties of interrupt gestures include just raising the hand a few inches, then letting it fall, placing fingers on the lips, or in extreme cases reaching out and touching the other person's forearm.

At the sign of these signals, you should be both elated and warned—heartened that others are at least listening to you but warned that they think it is time for them to have a turn.

Be alert for the red light! It is heralded by a silence—a stony silence. The hostess retreats to the kitchen to check on the coffee; a couple of the guests set up their own little subgroup. Note the gestures. People in the party start positioning their bodies as if about to rise and get going. Their movement is saying, "It's late and we'd better be going on our way." Some people are so polite that when you say, "I hope you won't have to go early," they respond, "Oh, we're only going to stay for a little while." But if they continue to move toward the edge of the chair, they're giving you a nonverbal message that no matter what their lips are saying, they are anxious to be on their way. Bring your effort to a halt. Quit. Release your captives. Retain their goodwill. Let someone else take over.

ANOTHER JEWISH WIFE

Our ideal wife of a prominent politician of her day might have a special message for the wife of a Jewish political leader of our day. The husband of the ideal wife sat at the gate of the city among the political leaders, but his problems must have been elemental compared with the responsibilities of a modern Israeli leader. Being prime minister of Israel requires versatility and toughness as the occupant of that post guides a beleaguered nation surrounded by hostile countries, contends with the enormous financial clout of vengeful, oil-rich Arab neighbors, keeps together warring internal factions, and maintains good relations with America, whose financial assistance helps ensure survival.

Yitzhak Rabin brought to the job of prime minister a reputation as a tough-minded leader who guided his country through some of its most difficult years. After serving one successful term, Rabin decided to take advantage of the climate and resigned, expecting a relatively easy reelection campaign. But he had overlooked the influence of his wife, Lea.

An aggressive, Prussian-born immigrant to Israel, Lea established a reputation for her independent ways. In the midst of a hard-fought election campaign, it was revealed that the prime minister's wife had broken Israel's currency laws by maintaining an American bank account. Following the revelation, Rabin withdrew; but many Israelis signed petitions requesting him to reconsider his withdrawal. The reaction to his wife was far less favorable. She was unpopular because of the aggressive way she horned in on Rabin's activities. The most damning indictment of all was that she had corrected her husband while he was speaking to an American audience. She had failed to learn the lesson of the ideal wife as portrayed in Proverbs, "When she speaks her words are wise."

TIPS ON IMPROVING CONVERSATION

Let the other person save his face. People will often make foolish statements that are obviously incorrect; you do not have to put them right—keep *listening.*

Be pleasant and friendly as you talk and do not forget to *listen.*

If you have been fortunate in some area, do not talk too much about it. Envy is such a powerful reaction that if affects most people in their attitude toward you—ease off and *listen.*

The honest "I don't know" is often the best reply to some question about a matter in which your information is very limited—then *listen.*

People are always more interested in themselves than they are in you—*so listen* to them.

As the other person talks, formulate a question that will encourage him or her and then *listen* for the answer.

Play conversational tennis, seeing how adept you can become in hitting the conversational ball back and waiting for a return by *listening.*

Watch for warning signals—be sensitive to other people's reactions. If you are not doing so well, try *listening* for a while.

I love tennis. Openly and unashamedly, I am a nut, a tennis nut. I take advantage of every opportunity to play. The game brings with it an exhilaration, a feeling of well-being somewhat akin to a titillating conversation. This makes it natural for me to think of conversation as being like a game of tennis.

Look at the tennis player. In the process of learning to improve her game, she spends hours at the practice wall. She plays her strokes to the wall; and as the ball rebounds, she drives or smashes or lobs it back to the wall, from where it will return to her again. She plays to herself, as do many so-called conversationalists. Let us look in at the group gathered for coffee in the Storer home. As they sit around the room, Pat Storer looks across at Dorothy Seivers.

PAT: *I just love your pantsuit, Dorothy.*

DOROTHY: *Thank you. Jim, that's my husband, was telling me before he left for work this morning: "Make sure you wear your pantsuit. I think it does something for you." Of course, that's Jim; he's always saying something nice. You know, the other night I heard him talking to Mark, that's our fourteen-year-older; and he was saying, "If you can only get a girl like your mother, you will do remarkably well. . . ."*

So it goes on. Dorothy has to tell something about every member of her family—her children's achievements in school, her daughter's activities in the choir, her husband's travels, his long-distance call, the gifts he brings when he returns home, comments the neighbors have made on the Seivers's remarkable solidarity. Dorothy is a practice wall player in the conversation game. She keeps on hitting the ball against the wall in the hope it will return to her again. Henry Ford is credited with defining a bore as "someone who opens his mouth and puts his feats in it." Dorothy is a champion bore.

Contrast Dorothy with Mrs. Purvis, who plays the conversation game with the skill of a coach, making her strokes to provide the person on the other side of the net an opportunity to return the ball. As my husband and I drove to the Purvis home, I noted the pine trees and the carefully manicured lawns edged with azaleas. Henrietta Purvis was a rare spirit, a woman who had achieved in the largely masculine corporate world and held a high executive position in a nationally known fabric manufacturing firm. We braced ourselves for a prolonged discussion on the status of the fabric industry.

Sitting in her beautifully furnished living room, Mrs. Purvis opened the conversation by addressing my husband, "I seldom get a chance to talk with a psychologist. Could you tell a layperson something about sensitivity training and the theory of group therapy you have written about in your book?"

She had read his books. She knew of my work. Somehow she had learned of his interests and mine. She continued to hit the conversational ball back into our court. Like the skillful tennis instructor, this intelligent woman was giving us an opportunity to execute our best strokes. Small wonder my husband and I both felt warm toward her.

Beware of the smash. The smash is the lethal shot of tennis. One player sends the ball sailing slowly over the net; and the opponent sees the opportunity, rushes in for the kill, and smashes the ball down at a lightning speed that makes it impossible to return.

Downright contradiction is an example of a conversational smash. Like the aggressive tennis player, you may gain a moment of satisfaction; but you will successfully slow down, if not kill, any hope of conversation. The conversational Golden Rule is "SPEAK AS YOU WOULD LIKE TO BE SPOKEN TO."

Jean Garret has just arrived at the Caudle household, where she has been invited for dessert. Margie Caudle has introduced Jean around the group and says, "Jean is a systems analyst and is working at the new airport. Jean, why don't you tell us something about the new parking system?"

JEAN: They have devised a new way of parking your car so you just drive up, and you can get to the check-in counter within five minutes.

JANETA SIMPSON: Oh, yeah? That's the biggest lot of nonsense I ever heard. Airline propaganda, that's all that is. You can't put that over on an old pro like me. Why I remember. . . .

Janeta has scored a smash, but she has ruined the conversation and effectively squashed Jean. You do not have to be a "yes" woman. Janeta could have said, "I'll be happy to see that. I must confess I find it hard to believe." If you cannot agree with what is being talked about, you can say, "Well, I don't quite see it that way" or "Another way to look at it is this." Thus you keep the conversation moving along while injecting a new interesting idea that will stimulate rather than smash a conversation.

I love to join in conversation with others and I suppose I am, in John's words, "a born helper." If I am talking with someone who is having difficulty expressing herself, I have to fight the tendency to jump in and give an assist. Gradually, I am learning the best way to be a good conversationalist is to learn to listen. As I learn to listen, I develop a skill that helps me make a wise response when I speak; and in that way at least I am like superwife.

CHAPTER 18

A Model Mother

unning her household with efficiency, she shows the value of super-
vision and example.

Prov. 31:27

TZADI

Crammed in the stifling telephone booth of the air terminal
and caught in a maelstrom of emotions following a missed flight, I
struggled to catch the words of the party at the other end of the line
as he gave me the name of a man I must contact upon arrival at my
destination. I must remember that name. No paper or pencil available,
I mentally cast around for a way to tie down that all-important appella-
tion. Then I recalled a technique of which I had once heard. Make an
association—the more incongruous and farfetched, the better. The
man's name was Mr. Phil Hatcher. I visualized a tall thin woman
swallowing (filling herself, fill with) a hatchet (fill—hatchet-her). Arriving at my destination, I strolled up to the paging counter and confidently said, "Please page Mr. Phil Hatcher."

I had learned to use a mnemonic device to help me remember. There
are many of these learning aids; some people use such simple techniques as rhyming or associated words. One of the oldest and most
widely used techniques for recalling a series of items is to begin each
one with a successive letter of the alphabet. This type of device was
used in biblical times, and Proverbs 31 is a classical example of it. The
mnemonic device helped little Hebrew girls memorize the passage so

they would know how the ideal woman lived, loved, and acted. As an interesting sidelight, we might note one missionary girls' organization today has the girls pass through a number of steps. One of these steps is to memorize Proverbs 31, probably with the idea that a developing adolescent girl, easily captured by idealism, would have an example of the life she should aspire to.

MODELING

The word "teach" means to show, and the best teaching is frequently done by demonstrating. So has come a concept of teaching sometimes referred to as "imitative learning," "observational learning," or "modeling." Traditionally, we have stated people learn by trial and error; but we know there are many skills, such as swimming, automobile driving, and performing surgery, that cannot be learned this way. In each of these instances, the student needs to watch someone else perform the skill before trying it.

Of course, the method is not really new. Jesus Christ was a great example. He took a basin and towel and washed his disciples' feet. When he was finished, he said, "If I then, your Lord and Master, have washed your feet, ye ought also to wash one another's feet. I have given you an example that ye should do as I have done to you" (John 13:14–15).

In the New Testament, there is what the Scottish theologian William Barclay calls the ethic of imitation.[1] Christians are told to be imitators of God: "Be ye therefore followers of God, as dear children" (Eph. 5:1). They are also exhorted to imitate Christ: "For even hereunto were ye called: because Christ also suffered for us, leaving us an example, that ye should follow His steps" (1 Pet. 2:21). Great personalities of the Christian faith are also to be imitated by Christians: "Consider the outcome of their life and imitate their faith" (Heb. 13:7). Paul uses the idea of modeling in his teaching ministry and frequently tells the Christians to imitate him: "I urge you to be imitators of me" (Phil. 3:17). "Be imitators of me as I am of Christ" (1 Cor. 11:1). Paul exhorts leaders: "Don't be tyrants but lead them by your good example" (1 Pet. 5:3). The New Testament has anticipated many modern educational procedures and has a lot to say about what one authority calls "imitative learning."[2]

However, the New Testament knew nothing about a new type of imitative learning that has been called "symbolic modeling." In symbolic modeling the subject sees an action on a movie screen or television and so learns a behavior. On May 24, 1978, a personable woman chartered a helicopter to fly her from St. Louis, Missouri, to Cape Girardeau, Missouri. As they flew over the countryside, the woman told the pilot she was the mother of five and had worked as an air traffic controller. As they approached Marion, Illinois, the woman reached over, tore off the pilot's microphone, produced a pistol, and ordered him to fly to a maximum security prison, land the helicopter, and pick up three waiting convicts. The whole dramatic event ended in tragedy as the pilot struggled with and finally shot the would-be skyjacker.

Later reports indicated the method was not as novel as many might imagine. It had been used in *Breakout,* a movie that had been aired on television. The story concerned just such a helicopter jailbreak. Further investigation revealed that since the airing of the movie there had been at least three jail break attempts using the same idea. Television, that superb teacher, had used symbolic modeling to teach desparate convicts how to make a jailbreak.

Modeling techniques are generally used unconsciously as a teaching method. Those involved do not realize they are modeling, and some of the models we have considered have been bad models. How can we effectively use modeling as a method of teaching good, wholesome skills that will improve the individual's ability to cope with life? Four factors go into making a good modeling technique: an attentive student, adequate demonstrations, guided practice, and success experiences.

Attention is always a factor in a teaching-learning situation. Every teacher knows how an inattentive student can deflate him and reduce his performance, but the student's attention is doubly important in modeling. If the student is not paying attention, all the modeling is in vain, for the whole experience depends upon the student's observation.

When a colleague of mine retired from his position as president of an educational institution, his friends arranged for him to have his portrait painted by the famous Australian artist Joshua Smith. Joshua Smith had gained many honors because of his portrait painting skills, and my friend was flattered to have such a noted artist do the portrait. He took particular note of the way Smith looked at him. For every five seconds the artist worked, he spent three looking and two painting. After fifteen hours of working, Smith said, "I saw you for the first time yesterday. I'm not satisfied and I want to start again." He continued; and when the painting was finished, my friend estimated the artist had looked at him over sixty-thousand times.

The amount of attention the learner pays to the model is important in determining the amount of learning that takes place.

The teacher should provide the student with a series of examples demonstrating how the particular skill is performed. The more examples provided, the better the possibility is for teaching.

A television nature program showed how Alaskan brown bears learn to hunt. It also showed a mother bear teaching her cubs to fish. She takes the baby bears to the rapids up which the salmon must swim in their migration to their birth place. The mother bear wades in and begins scooping up the fish. Watching mother at work, the cub soon plunges into the water and begins attempting to catch fish. When successful, he carries them ashore. At this time the small bears have no real taste for fish; they prefer their mother's milk. Once ashore with the fish, they are not quite sure what to do with it. Purely by imitation the small bears are learning a skill they will need to survive.

Sometimes modeling is done more subtly. A concerned mother had talked to the school speech pathologist about some of her daughter's speech problems. The therapist gave the mother some coaching on how to help her daughter pronounce the word "drink," which Patty produced as "dink." The speech teacher said, "When your daughter says 'dink,' you immediately take up the conversation: 'Would you like a *drink?'*—very clearly and distinctly—I like to *drink* water; do you like to *drink* water? What would you like to *drink* at supper time tonight?" Patty's mother had given her a series of models to encourage the little girl to pronounce at least one word correctly.

Having observed the model in action, the would-be learner needs guided practice to develop the skill. I once tried my hand at wood carving. The whole idea had appealed to me for a long time; so I bought books and tried to follow the directions, with scant success. Then I made contact with a man who was willing to give me some lessons. I commenced by watching him in action and immediately could see where I had made some rather obvious mistakes. Then I tried. My teacher would periodically stop me and demonstrate and let me try again. I shall never become a Michelangelo, but I did some passable work.

Modeling can also be helpful in changing behavior, as the case of Mrs. Willis shows. Mrs. Willis is a fifty-four-year-old little girl. She sat and chewed gum while she talked to her therapist in a childish voice and periodically shrugged her shoulders in despair and asked, "What should I do?" Further discussion revealed her husband had been a paternal guide in her life, looking after all the family affairs, making decisions, and writing all the checks. The children were now grown, and Mrs. Willis suspected her husband was having an affair with another woman.

When she would discover some definite evidence of her husband's involvement, she characteristically reacted by moving home to mother, where she poured out the story of her husband's transgressions. Her family treated her like their favorite "little girl" and immediately urged her to divorce her faithless husband. Now Mrs. Willis was having some second thoughts as she faced the reality of living as a lonely, fifty-four-year-old divorcee with no marketable occupational skills. She decided to meet with a counselor.

The counselor noted her teenage outfit, her juvenile jewelry, and the way she curled up in a large chair and spoke in a plaintive voice as if she were pleading with her grandfather to do something with her naughty husband. The counselor helped his client explore her potential strategies and their possible outcomes. She finally decided living at home with her mother was not the solution and she needed to make a move toward reconciliation. But how would she go about it? She shrugged her shoulders helplessly.

The counselor realized his client had a lot of learning to do and went into action. He commenced by showing the way she came across to a man. A fifty-four-year-old little girl was an anomaly. He suggested a way she could approach her husband and said, "Let's imagine you are your husband and I am you." He then began, "Honey, I want to talk with you . . ." and proceeded with the line he wanted her to follow. Then he restructured the scene: "Now let's pretend I am your husband. Tell me what you're going to tell him."

Her first effort was pathetic. She spoke like a kindergartener reciting lines. When she was finished, the counselor commended her effort but pointed out some of its weaknesses. The counselor now played her role again and repeated the statement the way he wanted her to do it. Then he reversed the roles to play the part of her husband while she tried again. The process was slow and time consuming; but when Mrs. Willis left the office, she had a changed bearing and an air of confidence as she went off to try out her newly acquired skill.

Possibly the most dramatic demonstration I ever saw of imitative learning was in Florence, Italy. As we wandered through one of the museums, my attention was attracted to the large number of would-be painters positioned before many of the classical art works, sitting in front of an easel, palette in one hand, brush in the other, copying the masterpiece.

I was told museum authorities make special provisions for budding artists to copy the masterpieces, insisting only that they not be done in the original size. As the tourists wandered by examining the paintings, many of them also looked at the work of the apprentice artists. Most of these tourists were relatively unsophisticated in the realm of art, and it was interesting to hear their comments: "Looks just like the original." "I see we have another Reubens." "I think yours is an improvement on the original." It is not difficult to see how students would be encouraged in developing their painting skills.

AN ASSORTMENT OF SKILLS

We have previously noted superwife was an actionist, constantly on the move. It is not just action for action's sake. Her life was lived at a purposeful level as she busied herself with many worthwhile tasks. As she worked, she demonstrated a whole series of skills, as described in various verses of Proverbs 31:

1. Relating to and being a partner to her husband [v. 16]
2. Becoming interested and developing a hobby [v.13]
3. Studying and providing for the nutritional needs of her family [v. 14]
4. Developing good routines and habits of life [v. 15]
5. Acting energetically and finding the satisfaction of zestful living [v. 17]
6. Buying wisely by comparison shopping [v. 18]
7. Helping poor people by giving gifts and showing compassion [v. 19]
8. Planning ahead in all the activities for the family [v. 21]
9. Sewing and making clothes and household decorations [v. 22]
10. Running a business [v. 24]
11. Communicating with her family [v. 26]

The demonstration of her expertise in so many areas probably caused mothers to point to superwife as a lesson for their daughters and as an example of the sort of wife their sons should seek later in life.

Sarah Edwards would have understood superwife in her role as a model. When Sarah married Jonathan Edwards, she became the wife of one of the more verbose Puritan preachers and soon discovered some of the peculiar responsibilities of a preacher's wife. During the church service, she occupied a special high bench positioned so she faced the congregation. She became the model for the other members of that congregation. Others might nod or nap during preaching, but she must remain the alert listener through the whole lengthy sermon. Like superwife, she showed the value of example. As an old Jewish proverb says, *"What the daughter does her mother did."*

CHAPTER 19

Children, Children, Children

he receives commendation from her children and rejoices as they
stand up and bless her.

Prov. 31:28

QOF

It is easy to see this verse was written a long time ago. Her
children stand up and bless her. How quaint. If it had been written
today and the writer had the benefit of our psychological studies and
had lived through the turbulent sixties, he would have known that most
of our adult problems result from what our mothers did to us during
infancy and childhood. One young woman said of her mother, "She
should love me no matter what; she should put me before her husband.
I need love; that's why I hate her, I hate her, I hate her." As one
perceptive woman wrote, "It seems as if we have raised a generation
of parent-hating children." If Proverbs 31 were written today, it would
probably read, "Her children bless her *out.*"

A university president disclosed a remarkably effective training
method that does not utilize buildings, athletic fields, tenured professors, or any type of organized curriculum. Daniel R. Grant, president
of Ouchita Baptist University, writing a guest editorial, told the secret
of his early education at home. The youngest of five children, he had
the task of drying the dishes. As they moved through the piles of dishes,
his mother discussed a variety of subjects, including the events of the

day and principles of human relations, all laced with a good measure
of practical Christianity. Dr. Grant describes the curriculum:

> I did not know it at the time, but I learned some invaluable lessons from
> Mother while drying dishes, and most of them were simply through observ-
> ing over and over again the way she thought and spoke in response to my
> childish questions. I think I learned to beware of "snap judgments," or of
> pre-judging something or somebody without adequate evidence or informa-
> tion, primarily because she was so careful to avoid snap judgments. I think
> I learned to be more careful and constructive in my criticisms. . . . I was in
> the classroom with one of the finest teachers anyone could have. Would I
> have missed all this if there had been an electric dishwasher in our kitchen
> during my childhood?[1]

During a discussion of the relationship of parents and children, one
woman said, "Do you know what has caused this situation? You profes-
sionals can come up with all sorts of fancy explanations, but as I see
it the problem is dishwashers. Yes, that's right, dishwashers. When we
had to wash our dishes by hand, it was a team effort. One would wash,
another rinse, and a third dry. The kids would complain and often fight
each other. But we'd also talk. Now we've got a dishwasher there's no
regular time when we can get together."

She may have a point. In one type of group therapy, each participant
answers the question, "Which was the warmest room in your house?"
Almost invariably the answer is the kitchen. The kitchen has traditionally been the focal point of family life. Actor Peter Falk once said, "I
don't go to nobody's home. I'm not comfortable sitting in living rooms.
I happen to like the kitchen better." With the kitchen no longer a
gathering place, it becomes a lonely spot for a housewife.

THE SUSANNA METHOD

Superwife in her relationship with her children surely set the pace
for mothers. At one gathering of husbands and wives where this passage
of scripture was read, a man raised his voice in angry complaint, "No
woman could be that good." But one scholar thinks so. John A. Newton, commenting on Proverbs 31:28, says of one woman, "She came

as near embodying this scripture ideal of the good wife and mother as mortal woman has ever done."[2] The woman is Susanna Wesley, an eighteenth-century example of a mother in action.

Mothers need help. Parenting is one of the most complex and difficult tasks an individual can attempt; and it is doubly difficult for the mother, whose life is inextricably bound up with the children she has borne. Where is she to find assistance for this difficult task? A concerned mother may turn to some system to help her cope with her maternal responsibilities. Many methods are available—the Ginot method, the Spock method, the Piaget method, the Gesell method-but what about the Susanna method?

The Susanna method produced a large family that included such notables as John Wesley, sometimes called the greatest Englishman of the eighteenth century, and Charles Wesley, the writer of over five thousand hymns. Of this family it was said, "They had the common fame of being the most loving family in the county of Lincoln."[3] Some would not limit this to Lincoln.

The mother of this family had a wide experience in family life, being one of twenty-five children herself. She bore nineteen children. Wife of a Church of England minister, Susanna managed on an inadequate salary, looked after the glebe lands belonging to the rectory, took her part in parish activities, and for twenty years ran what to some must have been a full-time school.

To further complicate their situation, the Wesleys lived in Epworth, located in the fen country, a land of swamps and canals where the people were benighted, suspicious, and found it difficult to accept their educated rector and his ever-increasing family.

In one parish squabble an enraged parishioner insisted on immediate payment of a debt. Reverend Wesley, being unable to pay, was arrested and placed in a debtor's prison in Lincoln Castle; and Susanna had to take over the responsibilities of the home. The cows were wounded, so that source of food was cut off. Reverend Wesley had to provide his own food in jail, and Susanna was reduced to sending him her rings to buy sustenance to keep him alive. Yet Susanna proved herself sufficient for this and myriad other crises she faced.

Preeminently, she was a mother. Of the nineteen children she bore, only ten survived to adulthood; but with these ten she established a remarkable record by using what she called "my method" which we shall call "the Susanna method." Looking back at Susanna, one of her grandsons commented, "She had the happy talent of imbuing a child's mind with every kind of useful knowledge in such a way as to stamp it on the memory."[4] An examination of her teaching methods shows the correctness of this grandson's judgment. She was a remarkable educator and used a no-nonsense technique. When a child reached five years of age, the process began. The school day was six hours long, from nine to twelve with a break, then from two to five.

The household was ordered so no one would interrupt the process, and the children settled down to work. She taught her pupils the alphabet, "letters great and small," in one day. She noted ruefully in one letter that Molly and Nancy took a day and a half to accomplish this, and she considered them dull. As soon as the child learned the alphabet, Susanna sat him down before a Bible opened at the first chapter of Genesis. She taught him a word at a time until he could read the whole verse. This procedure was then repeated a number of times to make sure he had really grasped it. Then he moved on until the whole chapter was finally completed.

In a society where it has been said a modern parent never hits a child except in self-defense, Susanna's ideas about discipline probably sound rather rigid and harsh. After the manner of her times, she was a strict disciplinarian and set up a series of specific conditions for her children.

1. Even as babies they were taught to cry softly.
2. The children had to eat whatever was put before them. She noted a dividend from this. When the children had to take unpleasant medicine, they managed it nicely without complaint.
3. They were not allowed to eat or drink between meals.
4. All the children were to be in bed by 8 P.M. and were left in their room even if awake. No one sat with them until they went to sleep.
5. Each child had to be obedient. Susanna considered self-will the root of all sin and misery.

6. Once the child had been punished, the event was forgotten and never held against him.[5]

Susanna obviously went along with the writer of the book of Proverbs, who stated, "He that spareth the rod hateth his son" (Prov. 13:24).

However, in some ways Susanna's method of handling her children sounds like the modern techniques of behavior modification, which have shown behavior to be carried on in terms of its consequences. If a child cries and is placated, it soon learns the lesson—crying brings rewards. Susanna anticipated this, and she laid down the principle, "If they cried they would *not* receive what they wanted.[6]

This perceptive woman also noticed how children were unwittingly taught to be deceitful. When a child committed some undesirable act, he was faced with a dilemma. If he admitted the act, he was punished; so he learned to be deceitful. Susanna laid down a principle: "That whosoever was charged with a fault of which they were guilty, if they would ingeniously confess it, and promise to amend, *should not be beaten.*"[7] This wise woman used consequences to help build honesty into her children's lives.

Susanna was a gifted teacher, and part of her success came from her patience and willingness to repeat things many times. On one occasion, her husband was watching her at work with the children and actually counted the number of times she repeated a piece of information to the same child. Samuel, who had a very impatient, nature, marveled. At length he could stand it no longer and commented, "I wonder at your patience, you have told that child twenty times the same thing." Susanna calmly replied, "If I had satisfied myself by mentioning it only nineteen times I should have lost all my labor. It was the twentieth time that crowned it."[8] Long before professional educators had taught the idea, Susanna had learned that repetition breeds retention.

Despite her large brood of children, child raising was never a mass-production effort for Susanna. She was very concerned about the individual child and tried to show how life had something to teach each one of them. In one of her most moving statements, Susanna described her method for ensuring each child its fair share of attention. "I observe the following method. I take such a proportion of time I can spare every night to discourse with each child. On Monday I talk with Molly; Tuesday with Hetty; Wednesday with Nancy; Thursday with Jacky; Friday with Patty; Saturday with Charles; and with Emily and Sukey together on Sunday."[9]

A CONTINUING INFLUENCE

Susanna's method kept her an influence in her children's lives right through their adult lives, and this was particularly seen with John. When John faced the challenge as to whether he should go to America to minister in the new colony established by Oglethorpe, he consulted his mother. Her response: "If I had twenty sons I should rejoice if they were all so employed though I never saw them anymore."[10] So John and Charles Wesley went to Georgia.

Following the Wesleys' return to England to John's "heartwarming experience" in Aldersgate Street, the Wesleys launched a great crusade, now sometimes called the Evangelical Revival. And Susanna played her part.

Susanna's husband had died, her children were all grown, but her influence continued. During the first forty years of married life, she had hardly stirred out of Epworth; but now, in the "empty nest" years, she spread her wings and moved around. John Wesley established himself in an old building called the Foundery. It was used for church services and the activities of the people called Methodists. Susanna joined him and became a spiritual guiding force in her sons' lives. Some of John Wesley's major decisions in this new Methodist movement were made under his mother's influence.

Wesley made wide use of groups, variously called the class meeting, bands, or select society. This process probably stemmed from his family experiences and his mother's love of getting groups of people together, as did his use of women in leadership positions within the groups. Susanna took an active interest in the groups in the Foundery, and her example may have paved the way for the wide use of women as leaders. Susanna also played an important part in John Wesley's decision to use laymen in the work of his societies, the move that made Methodism a trailblazer as a major religious group.

During the Wesley brothers' absences from the Foundery, Thomas Maxfield, a layman, arranged the meetings of the societies and the bands. He could not preach because this activity was reserved for ordained priests. On one occasion the preacher failed to show and Maxfield took the pulpit.

When he returned to the Foundery, John heard the news and decided to rebuke Maxfield. It was Susanna who declared, "He is as surely called to preach as you are."[11] After hearing Maxfield, John agreed and began to use lay preachers more extensively.

Susanna Wesley is known because of her renowned sons. And that is the way she would have wanted it. As she said in a letter to her husband, "I cannot but look upon every soul you leave under my care as a talent committed to me under trust by the great Lord of all families."[13]

CHAPTER 20

The Making of an Ideal Wife

ribute comes from her husband; he says, "There are many fine women in the world, but you are the best of them all."

Prov. 31:29

RESH

Walking out on family responsibilities used to be almost solely a male prerogative. Desertion was said to be "a poor man's divorce," and many men elected this method of terminating a marriage. Things are rapidly changing. A fifty-year-old firm specializing in locating missing people reports that in 1960 there were three hundred requests to trace runaway husbands for every one request to search for a missing wife. By 1974, the number of runaway wives was slightly higher than the number of runaway husbands. The ratio had changed from three hundred to one in 1960 to one to one in 1974.

Why did these wives leave home? There are many reasons, but at least one authority points out that many wives who left home returned later, leading him to conclude that running away from home was a cry for help. He adds, "Women are really demanding attention from their husbands who have forgotten everything about them—even the color of their eyes."

All people need attention. Something within us cries out for recognition. Michelangelo worked for two years on the *Pieta*. After its completion, he and his friends painstakingly struggled to transport and place the statue in St. Peter's Cathedral. The sculptor, who had put so much of his life into the statue, awaited the viewers' response. On Sunday he joined a group of people standing around the *Pieta* and listened to them speculating about the name of the sculptor. His heart sank as he heard no mention of his own name. That night Michelangelo took a bag of tools and a candle, crept into the great church, and went into action. The following day visitors to the statue read the words he had chiseled on the marble band that ran across the Virgin's chest: "Michelangelo Buonarroti of Florence Made This."

The human desire for recognition may help explain how women develop their potentialities. Superwife in Proverbs may be the product of the implementation of some laws of behavior. These laws have been practiced for many years, but only recently have they been systematically formulated and consciously applied. Central to these laws is attention.

CHANGING BEHAVIOR

One old wisecrack is, "I think I'll trade mamma in on a new model." The fact is a man can get a new wife without getting into the complications involved in "trading" simply by using a strategy that develops and highlights her potentialities. This involves knowing what researchers have discovered about the basis for human behavior and utilizing this knowledge. Many men want to change their wives, but they go about it the wrong way.

Henry Higgins undertook the task of transforming Eliza Doolittle from a dirty-faced flower girl into a beautiful woman who would be accepted as a royal princess. As *My Fair Lady* progresses, Professor Higgins, the irascible teacher, cajoles, shouts, and demeans his student in an effort to remake her. He is so thoughtless of her feelings that when they return home after her triumph at the ball, he and his friend Colonel Pickering spend most of their time congratulating each other on the feat and completely ignoring Eliza. Humiliated by Higgins's attitude, Eliza gathers her possessions together and quietly slips away.

My Fair Lady is superb entertainment and I have seen it at least fifteen times. It carries a great message about the richness, use, and misuse of the English language; but as an illustration of how to change behavior, it is about as far from the mark as it is possible to be. It ignores the basic principle that if the greatest reward one person can give another is attention, then the greatest punishment is withdrawal of attention. Higgins constantly rewarded all the bad aspects of Eliza's speech by shouting about them. The situation was partially saved when Eliza managed to repeat perfectly, "The rain in Spain came mainly on the plain" and Higgins joyously sang, "I believe she's got it." But even then the commendation was short and soon forgotten. The play violates the basic principle of behavior changing, which is to ignore unwanted behavior and focus on desirable behavior.

The first ingredient in wife changing is to punish bad behavior. Punish it by ignoring it. In the poem of wifely excellence, the husband does not enumerate his wife's faults, suggesting she may be going overboard with all her activities. This woman must have had *some* faults; she was not perfect. Her husband was smart; he ignored her undesirable behavior and focused on her good points.

Attention is the greatest reward one individual can give another, and the highest form of attention is praise. Probably the most frequently heard complaint from troubled wives is that their husbands and families do not appreciate them, and their complaint is usually justified. One of Charles Dickens's characters telling his friend about his wife's unusual abilities, says, "But I never tells her." This is all too frequently the husband's attitude. Proverbs 27:5 speaks about the same principle: "Open rebuke is better than hidden love." It is impossible to be neutral about this. If a husband appreciates his wife but never tells her, he is punishing her by his silence.

Naturalists tell us all the pupa in a beehive are the same; but when the hive needs a new queen, the workers select one pupa and feed it the royal jelly. As the pupa is fed the royal jelly, it grows and develops in a distinctive way until it becomes a queen. The royal jelly that makes a queen out of an ordinary woman is praise. General praise is good, of course, but the most effective type of praise is descriptive.

NOT: You're a good wife.
BUT: I love the way you cooked that casserole and vegetables.

NOT: You're an excellent mother.

BUT: It was great to see the way you organized those kids and got them off to the picnic.

NOT: I can leave the budget in your hands.

BUT: I can't help but notice the way you keep the checkbook balanced and pay all the bills properly.

NOT: The house looks nice.

BUT: You certainly made the whole place more attractive when you rearranged the living room furniture.

Developing praise power is not easy; it may even need a plan of action. Some behavior shapers suggest keeping a daily record of praise statements made. The would-be praiser decides on a goal and move toward it. Each day he records how often he praised the person he is seeking to change. Some companies today are specializing in supplying premiums to firms that want to provide employee incentives. Interestingly, the best premium of all, praise, does not cost any money and is the most effective.

Susan Rockford, blonde, smartly dressed in tailored striped silk shirt and linen suit, voiced her major complaint about her executive husband. "When we are with a group of people and I make some mistake, he calls attention to it in front of everybody. I don't so much mind him telling me, but I don't want him telling me in front of all my friends. It's demeaning." Susan has voiced the concern of many wives for the way their husbands inflict social punishments upon them. However, the reverse is true. If a husband wants to reward his wife, the most effective way is in the presence of others. This adds the social factor to the reward.

The director of one of the first films David Niven ever made realized this. Niven, young and inexperienced, had been cast in the role of a poet. The script called for him to enter a long room full of people and move past the groups of characters, greeting the men, kissing the women, wisecracking, and generally being the life of the party. Vividly aware of his opportunity, Niven became nervous and apprehensive. When the moment arrived, he rushed through the door, tripped and almost fell, bumped into a large woman sitting in a chair, addressed himself to the wrong people, and finally staggered to the conclusion. To Niven's amazement, everyone on the set, actors, extras, cameramen, and workmen, burst into applause. The director, face beaming, rushed up to commend him on his performance. That was it, the director said; they had it all filmed. However, he went on, just in case the cameras may have missed something, they would try it again. Glowing with confidence from the director's praise and basking in the applause of the people on the set, Niven told himself it was easy; even at his worst he was a success. Running through the scene the second time, he never missed a beat, played the part with cool aplomb, and turned in a perfect performance.

Later a friend who had been present told Niven what had happened. Before the shooting of the first scene, the director had assembled all the people and told them about this young actor who was very nervous. He said they would have a dry run first with no film in the camera and no matter how bad Niven was he would commend him and they should applaud. The social reinforcement had completely changed Niven.

Husbands must learn that when they compliment their wife, the size of the audience is always a basic consideration. The formula is $P \times A = E$. In this formula praise (P) is rendered increasingly effective (E) in a constant ratio to the size of the audience (A) before whom it is given.

In one form of therapy, a person with a low self-image is asked to sit in the center of the group. The other group members proceed to give this person a "strength bombardment," sometimes called "verbal gifts." Each tells something they like about the person. The superwife of Proverbs 31 was the subject of verbal bombardment. A whole series of groups praised her:

1. *The community.* "She shall be greatly praised" [v. 30].
2. *The leaders.* "These good deeds of hers shall bring her honor and recognition from even the leaders of the nation" [v. 31].
3. *Her family.* "Her children stand up and bless her, so does her husband" [v. 28].
4. *Her husband.* "He [her husband] praises her with these words,

'There are many fine women in the world but you are the best
of them all' " [v. 29].

Small wonder this woman became a superwife.

NEW WIVES FOR OLD

We can have better wives if we really want them. From our basic
assumption that attention is the greatest reward that can be given and
withdrawal of attention is the greatest punishment, we can formulate
a plan of action for changing wives. It will not be easy; any plan of
behavior changing is difficult. But it can be both productive and satisfying. A program will move through four levels, each of which calls for
skills a husband needs to develop.

The first level is looking. A woman in a counseling center explained
why she had slashed both her wrists in a suicide attempt: "I was trying
to get his attention." This is rather drastic; but some wives have to walk
out, file for divorce, fly off the handle, or bang up the automobile in
a costly attempt to get attention. There must be a better way. Watch
romantic lovers as they sit with their eyes focused on each other. It
makes both of them feel good to be on the center of somebody's stage.

One wife rushed up to her husband as he entered the house and
barked at him in imitation of the dog to which he generally gave his
attention first. The wife of a physician appeared at his office with $15
in hand and stated she was willing to pay the cost of a regular office
visit if she could have fifteen minutes of his time.

A good wife changer will examine his wife carefully, her dress,
hairdo, complexion, and eyes, and let her know he is vividly aware of
her presence and will praise her in descriptive detail.

The second level is listening. If attention is the great reward one
person can give another, then listening is a heightened form of attention and obviously one of the best techniques for reinforcing another
person's behavior. Does this sound too simple?

Listening is not easy. It is one of the most difficult skills to master.
My wife will vouch for this. We attended a conference in the course
of which I had to make five presentations in one day. Following the

evening effort, we returned to the motel room; and I flopped into a comfortable chair and tried to regroup my dwindling energies. "Why don't we go down to the coffee shop and have a dish of ice cream?" Robina suggested. Filled with self-pity, I was not too amenable to this suggestion and complained, "I can't be bothered. It's alright for you; I'm worn out. I had to speak five times today." Quick as a wink she rejoined, "What's wrong with you? I had to listen five times today."

She was right. Listening is often far more difficult than talking; and it requires determination, energy, and discipline to attain the skill.

Level three is concerned questioning. Some questions can be instruments of punishment. A mother quizzing her daughter coming in late at night or a district attorney with a hostile witness in court is going to evoke an admission. But this is not the task of a husband trying to change his wife; you are here to help your subject. Your question is a coaxing invitation for her to respond. An imaginative question can help immeasurably.

The late President Kennedy was widely known for his witty answers to questions fired at him at press conferences. He also could ask incisive questions and pay unusual attention to what was said to him. Robert Saudek conferred with the president while producing the television series, "Profiles in Courage." He later reported, "He made you think he had nothing else to do except ask you questions and listen—with extraordinary concentration—to your answers."[3]

Work on your ability to use that evocative question; it will greatly improve your effectiveness as a change agent.

The fourth level four is upgrading your praise capacity. If you have worked conscientiously on looking, listening, and questioning, you are ready for the next phase. This will involve techniques of looking for something to praise rather than criticize, making your praise descriptive, preparing for the task, and undertaking a training program using some of the methods we have already discussed.

I have often pondered Proverbs 31:29 and must keep reminding myself it is from the Old Testament. After many years of study, I have concluded the passage is far removed from the general tone of the Old Testament writings, which generally exalts the male and says men are superior to women. How can there be such a glorification of womanhood amid these writings that place woman in a secondary role in life? I have often thought the passage might be a plot by some determined group of women to propagandize the society of their day and create a new image of women's skills and abilities.

Perhaps this passage is from the pen of some manipulating male. Perhaps Solomon in all his wisdom and insights into human nature decided to produce a whole new crop of superior women. How could he do it? By praising them. So he wrote this lauditory passage that would so warm the hearts of women that they would put forth their best efforts and become the strength of his kingdom.

Proverbs 31:29 has always been a favorite with me. When I read the passage about this outstanding woman, I am filled with awe and admiration that she should have possessed so many gifts and capacities. Second thoughts about her and all she did have caused me to notice she had an unusual husband, and this might be more than half the reason she was successful.

As I have read, considered, and spoken about this passage, another thought has come into my mind; I wonder how superwife responded to her husband's statements. I am sure she did not say, "You're putting me on." or "What do you want?" or "You've got to be kidding." She must have responded wisely and so encouraged her husband to continue to make the statements she really liked to hear.

Having watched the way some women respond to a compliment, I would like to make six suggestions about how to respond to positive feedback. First, do not feel compelled to "trade." Although you should be ready to return a compliment, to indicate you are not so self-centered that you do not see something of value in the person who is complimenting you, it is not an absolute necessity. You can accept the compliment in the sincere spirit in which it is offered and simply say "thank you."

Second, never deny the statement. There is nothing more devastating than to have a compliment refused. It is rather like feeding an animal that bites your hand. Harriet Nelson took this attitude. As she sat in a group one evening lamenting her lack of ability, she happened to mention she was working on a new piece of needlepoint. The women in the group all expressed an interest, so the following week Harriet turned up with her needlepoint in hand. Irene Tims, accomplished at embroidery, said, "That's an excellent job. I can see you've put in a lot of time on it." Harriet replied, "Oh, come on, be honest. It's amateurish and you know it."

Harriet has embarrassed Irene, who was trying to encourage a newcomer to the field in which she herself had some expertise. How could Harriet have responded? One possibility is, "I appreciate a compliment from an expert like you. You encourage me."

Third, look upon positive feedback as a gesture of goodwill and respond accordingly. The old-fashioned meaning of "compliment" is a gift someone gave an inferior. Many of us feel demeaned when someone gives us something, much like a gratuity might appear to a servant. Let us take a sensible view of ourselves. Do not underrate yourself. You have certain gifts and because of these you are entitled to appropriate appreciation.

My fourth suggestion is not to question the motives of the person who gives you positive feedback. In our competitive society we are all too used to people softening us up before trying to get something from us. I know when someone compliments me, especially if he tends to be effusive, I wonder if he has an ulterior motive. Is he setting me up to make a sale? But he may be a person of goodwill who is sincerely trying to encourage me in something I am undertaking. I should accept his compliment at face value and not have some paranoid suspicion that he is trying to get to me.

Fifth, do not let the fear of criticism deny you the right to positive feedback. One of the best techniques of criticism is to find something to commend before you criticize. We have all had contact with people who use the technique of paving the way for criticism by complimenting, "This is very good, but. . . ." So when we hear a compliment, we may steel ourselves. But the person giving us positive feedback may have had no idea at all of being critical. Do not rush out to meet criticism halfway.

And finally, do not be too naive. Some people like to give a compliment. I once had a student in one of my classes who came up after every class with a beaming smile and excitedly said, "Oh, that was so wonderful. *Your lectures are so marvelous." I hope they were marvelous to her—but I am realist enough to know my utterances are not always inspired; in fact, some of them are very mediocre. As one actor said about applause, enjoy it but never quite believe it. Make a realistic evaluation of yourself.*

CHAPTER 21

The Beauty Queen

 nimpressed by flattering talk and superficial beauty, she knows true values lie in a reverential trust in her creator.

Prov. 31:30

SHIN

As a concession to feminists' criticisms, the promoters of a beauty contest held several years ago decided to introduce a segment designed to show the contestants could utter at least a short sentence. In the quiz, billed a test of mental alertness and capacity for self-expression, Penny Johnson was asked what three things every woman should covet most. Having been carefully drilled beforehand, Penny assumed a sweet expression and in her best girl-next-door voice said, "A good personality, an attractive appearance, and a finely tuned sense of values." The crowd applauded and her coach sighed with relief.

Although Penny saw herself as a thoroughly modern woman and felt her attitude indicated her modernity, these three aspects of femininity —charm, beauty, and a sense of values—are precisely the qualities set out in the thirtieth verse of our poem.

CHARM

The book of Proverbs tells about several types of women. Some were very unattractive and some were beautiful. The beautiful ones fell into two categories; some who are prominently mentioned use their charms as a means of exploiting other people. Solomon warns his son about a certain type of woman by citing an instance, "She seduced him with her pretty speech, her coaxing and her wheedling" (Prov. 7:21, LB). But there were other types of charming women, among them the good wife, of whom he says, "Rejoice in the wife of thy youth. Let her charms and tender embrace satisfy you" (Prov. 5:19, LB).

Superwife, busily engaged in the world of commerce, knew how people use their charm in business. Among the many people who give us trouble in our society today none is more difficult than the sociopath who is generally described as having a shallow emotional life, living in the area of immediacy without anticipating the future, never learning from experience but repeating the same self-defeating behavior, and given to exploiting other people for his own selfish ends. Superwife had probably met such people; earlier in Proverbs one is mentioned: " 'Utterly worthless!' says the buyer as he haggles over the price. But afterwards he brags about his bargain" (Prov. 20:14). As translated in the Living Bible, this verse brings a warning, "Charm can be deceptive." How was she to discriminate between the genuine charmer and the sociopath?

A clue to superwife's perceptiveness may be found in the twenty-first letter of the Hebrew alphabet, with which this verse commences. The consonant called shin—pronounced sheen—is like the Roman letter *s* which can be pronounced *sh* as in *sure* or *s* as in *son*. Shin is pronounced *sh* in one form and in a second form, called sin, is pronounced *s*. However, the Hebrews differentiate the pronunciation by the position of a dot: שׁ = shin and שׂ = sin. This simple change in the Hebrew letter is dramatized in one of the most colorful stories of the Old Testament.

In one of the factional fights that characterized the Old Testament tribes, the Ephraimites and Gileadites had a falling out. Jeptha, leader of the Gileadites, organized his men into an army and launched an attack on the men of Ephraim. His attack was so successful that he bottled up the Ephraimites and mounted guards on the only fords where they could possibly cross the River Jordan. But how to tell friend from foe? Jeptha's plan hinged on a peculiarity of Gileadite speech. In much the same way as few Americans can pronounce the guttural sound *ch* as do the Scottish, the Gileadites always used the alternative pronunciation of sin, making the *s* rather than the *sh* sound the Ephraimites favored.

As each man approached the ford, he was asked to pronounce the Hebrew word *shibboleth*—meaning corn. If he could not pronounce the *sh* sound and said *sibboleth,* he was identified as a Gileadite.

One dictionary gives the meaning of *shibboleth* as a password, but this was not originally so. It represented a way of pronouncing a Hebrew consonant. The questioner had to be discriminating in deciding who was friend and who was foe. The ideal woman in our poem had to have similar powers of discrimination. One of the hallmarks of a mature woman is her recognition that charm can have lethal possibilities and can be used to manipulate and defraud others. She has the ability to choose between the genuine and the counterfeit charm and to use her own personal charms creatively.

BEAUTY

Touring Rome some years ago, I visited the Church of San Pietro, where Michelangelo's remarkable statue of Moses sits, complete with a coin arrangement allowing camera-carrying tourists to drop in money and unleash a mercifully short glare of lights that causes bystanders to reel back and cover their eyes but enables the shutterbugs to take their pictures.

The impressive figure sits with straight back, flowing beard, raven looks, right arm firmly embracing the tablets of the law. But what are those two bumps protruding from the curly hair on the front of his head? I later discovered the bumps are, of all things, "horns." Why were there horns on the head of the man who had just descended from his conversation with God and was about to deliver the tablets of the law to the children of Israel waiting at the foot of the mountain?

Michelangelo was the victim of a Bible translator named Saint Jerome, who had made a Latin translation of the original Hebrew. The Hebrew words for "shine" and "horn" are nearly alike, *garan* and *geren,* and easily confused. Saint Jerome chose to read the word as *geren,* which he translated "horns" and so made the passage read,

"Moses knew not that his face was horned." Michelangelo in turn perpetuated and dramatized the error in his remarkable sculpture. From the context and other references in the Bible, we know it should be "Moses did not know that the skin of his face shone" (Exod. 34:29). Moses' face had upon it a beauty that comes from being in the presence of God.

Like Jerome, some of us see the wrong thing when we look for beauty. The word beauty is used on only two occasions in the book of Proverbs, in verse 30 of chapter 31 and where a father is warning his son about prostitutes: "Don't lust for their beauty" (Prov. 6:23). Beauty and sexual stimulation are not the same.

Women can often make a much more realistic estimate of feminine beauty than can men, who are much more susceptible to the blandishments of a pretty face. Martin Luther, whose marriage was in the best traditions of the Reformation—he married Katie Van Bora because she was an ex-nun and needed a husband to care for her—warned the young people of his day about the superficial attraction of a pretty face. "You would gladly have a beautiful, good, and rich wife if you could. Indeed we really ought to paint you one with red cheeks and white legs! These are the best, but they usually cook poorly and pray badly."[1] He looked back to the stories of the Old Testament and wondered whether Jacob should have married the more beautiful Rachel when Leah would have been the more suitable wife for him. In the best puritanical tradition, spiritual depth and domestic skills were to be preferred over physical beauty.

Luther may have a point. Physical beauty is passing and sometime devalues character, which may be the most valuable aspect of human personality. At least partial confirmation of this comes from studies in which men who married beauty queens were asked, after a few years of marriage, what they thought about their wives. Most of them expressed disappointment.

Three words from our poems should be written in bronze: "Beauty doesn't last." Herein lies the tragedy of all this emphasis on the human form and its appearance. Other translations highlight these ideas of the transience of beauty: "Comeliness is a deception and beauty is a vain thing," "Beauty is a breath," "Charms may wane and beauty wither, keep your praise for a woman with brains."[2]

Are women of worth only when they are young and beautiful? Are their thoughts, ideas, and concepts of no value? Because a woman lacks a shapely figure or a pretty face, is she to be cast aside? Many women who left their mark on the world were far from attractive in appearance. Look at Golda Meir. A plain and ordinary looking grandmother, she was a great leader at the helm of her country in its hour of need. The really beautiful women are those who like superwife have left their mark by their actions rather than their physical appearance.

VALUES

The monuments of ancient Egypt represent the epitome of a magnificent bygone civilization. The Greeks called the orderly rows of pictures that adorned these monuments *hieroglyphics,* which means sacred or priestly carving and reflects the Grecian idea that they represented some secret magical wisdom known only by Egyptian priests. In 1798, Napoleon led a French expeditionary force that landed at Alexandria. The following year an engineer officer in Napoleon's army found a stone half buried in the mud near the Rosetta mouth of the Nile River. Called the Rosetta stone, it proved to be a decree carved by Egyptian priests to celebrate the crowning of Ptolemy V, ruler of Egypt from 203 to 181 B.C. The inscription is repeated in three forms of writing. The first line is hieroglyphics; the second is demotic, the popular language of Egypt in that day; and the third is Greek. Because the Greek language was well known, it was possible to interpret the hieroglyphics. In this way the whole body of rich inscriptions on ancient Egyptian monuments was opened up for scholars. The Rosetta stone was the key to it all.

What is the key to true beauty? It is certainly not the accident of genetics by which a woman happens to inherit a pretty face or a curvaceous figure. The key is character, and the inward peace manifests itself upon the countenance. Superwife's faith is indicated by several versions of Proverbs 31:30: "A woman who reveres the Lord, she shall be praised." "It is the God fearing woman who is honored." "A woman who fears and reverences God shall be greatly praised." "A woman who honors the Lord should be praised." Our paraphrase tries to catch the sense of the Hebrew, showing this type of beauty comes from "a reverential trust in her creator."

A few years ago I visited a church in Alabama. There was great excitement because a young lady who had served as a staff member during the summer was a contestant in the Miss Alabama beauty contest. Then came the news that she had won and for a year would serve as Miss Alabama. I was there on the Sunday evening the very beautiful girl stood before a crowded church to relate her experiences. As she neared the conclusion, she told of her commitment to the cause of Christ and then sang the lovely song, "I'd Rather Have Jesus." Like superwife, she had her priorities straight.

My husband worked as a pastor for some years, and the churches in which we worked were steeped in the puritanical tradition. There was a certain unfairness in their attitude toward women—the old double standard again. The men could dress in the most expensive suits, but the women did not wear makeup and their unadorned appearance did little for them. At one of our church camps, a visitor looked over our girls and remarked, "There aren't too many stunners among them, are there?"

Whenever I hear some preacher thundering about "painted face Jezebels," it makes me sick. I cannot help but notice his expensive suit and well-styled hair and wonder how he could be so hypocritical.

After we were married, John told me about the problem he had had with his fellow seminary students. In this rather puritanical setting, the generally accepted idea was that attractive women were not spiritually minded. After one social event, to which all the seminary students brought their girlfriends, a couple of John's fellow students took him off to one side. After commenting on my attractiveness, they solemnly asked if I was spiritually minded. John roared with laughter. He claimed that was the highest compliment they could have paid me.

Looking back on it all, I feel it was grossly unfair to treat women like this. How I envied the girls I worked with. I constantly wished I could make up my face. Thank goodness we live in a more enlightened time. Whenever I see a very attractive, well-dressed minister's wife, I am grateful we have put aside many of the strange attitudes of the past.

CHAPTER 22

Well-Deserved Praise

irtue is rewarded as she is praised for all her good works even by the leaders of the nation.

Prov. 31:31

TAV

The first thirty chapters of the book of Proverbs, when they discuss Hebrew life, focus mainly on the male: what he is like, temptations that beset him, how he should act, and the wisdom he needs to order his life. Nearly one-third of the book is given over to the subject of raising a Hebrew boy. Among the unsavory characters supposedly out to get him are unscrupulous businessmen, avaricious moneylenders, rapacious people of means, and women.

While all this attention is lavished on sons, nothing is said about daughters. Apparently their education is of no importance. The one woman who has a good notice is the Hebrew male's mother, and he is told of the importance of listening to her instructions. But it almost seems as if the only reason this good woman is mentioned is that she will be important in raising a male to take his place with the other masculine leaders of Hebrew society. The other women are circling like birds of prey. They will deceive him, spend his money, nag him, seduce him, and when he does marry one, he will have to be on his toes lest she carry on an illicit love affair.

In chapter 31 we are abruptly ushered into the presence of a striking woman. A man is mentioned on several occasions, but he is a minor character who happens to be the husband of this remarkable woman. She mixes and mingles with the men of her day as she buys wool and flax from the farmers and shepherds, haggles with traders over their imported foods, dickers with landowners in the course of buying property, bargains with the sellers in the marketplace, and strikes deals with Phoenecian traders who seek to purchase the beautiful belted garments she makes. Moving amid this male-dominated society, she came out on top in her dealings. This woman stands head and shoulders above the other characters in Proverbs.

The passage is the more remarkable because nowhere in the Scriptures is there a similar portrayal of an ideal man. It seems there is a determined woman trying to get her message across. The passage begins, "The wise sayings of King Lemuel taught to him at his mother's knee." She was using the oldest and most effective teaching institution known to humanity, a mother's knee. Someone recently spoke of the problems of American education. Schools with decreasing enrollments are costing more to operate, thus the comment, "There's much fat in American education." If you want to get an idea of how much, just compare by looking at the products and the costs of the most illustrious of all institutions, the academy of a mother's knee.

Superwife was an early example of that genre of women known as "Jewish mothers," women who generally get their ideas across come heaven or high water. Some scholars claim Lemuel, whose name means literally "dedicated to God," may be King Solomon, placing superwife in the company of the noble band of women like Hannah, who dedicated their children to God. Then she proceeded to pass on her ideas to him. One translation says, "The advice which his mother gave him." She was spreading her ideas into a wider society through her son.

Thus she stood in a succession of women who have used their family to get a message to the world. One outstanding modern American family is the Kennedys, who produced an ambassador (Joseph P.), an attorney general (Robert), a president (John F.), and a senator (Edward), as well as highly influential daughters. Of his mother, President Kennedy said, "She was the glue that held us together." Asked to evaluate her mission in life, the indomitable Rose, who had seen one son killed in action during World War II and two others slain by assassin's bullets, said, "I would rather be known as the mother of a great son or daughter than the author of a great book or the painter of a great masterpiece." Her children were her medium of expression.

The opening verse of chapter 31 also indicates words of the last chapter are an oracle and a prophecy. Prophets in the Old Testament performed two functions: forthteller and foreteller. The most prominent of these was the forthteller who spoke out against the injustices of his day, declaring what he believed God wanted done in national affairs and moves to be made to alleviate the lot of the poor and the oppressed. This may have been what superwife had in mind. It seemed to her women were treated unfairly and something should be done about it. Here she causes her son to paint a picture of a woman with unusual abilities and accomplishments to indicate how the traditional Jewish treatment of women kept that society from using one of its greatest assets: the skills and abilities of its women. It would be part of the protest literature of that day.

If we take the word "prophesy" in the more traditional way and see it as projecting what is going to happen in the future, she shows how the woman of tomorrow could move into society and become leaders. Women have moved into leadership roles that were formerly a male province. Israel, the modern descendant of superwife's society, became one of the first nations in the twentieth century to have a woman head of state. The most discouraging aspect of such a projection is that it has taken so long for it to be fulfilled.

It could also describe how a woman can turn an apparent disaster into a triumph, as superwife, laboring against the heavy odds of the masculine prejudices of her day, nevertheless emerges triumphant. In modern times, Claire Booth Luce had an analogous experience. Her husband, Henry Luce, already eminently successful as the publisher of *Time* magazine, planned to launch a new picture magazine called *Life*. Claire, a successful ex-editor of *Vanity Fair* with an interest in picture magazines, worked long and hard with him in planning for the new publication and had high hopes of a prominent position on the editorial staff.

Although Henry Luce owned the enterprise, he left its management in the hands of two men. As publication date drew near, the two executives invited Mr. and Mrs. Luce to a meal. Dressing for the event, Henry Luce suggested to his wife she would probably be invited to take an editorial position. Once the meal was over, however, the two hosts broke the news that for a variety of reasons, including her husband's ownership, they thought it would be a mistake to have Mrs. Luce on the staff. Claire could hardly believe her ears. After her first shock and a crying spell in her room, she calmly told her husband that it might be best if she did not participate in any way with the new venture in which she had done so much planning. Then she calmly announced she would take time out to write a play. The result was *The Women,* a clever satire of the wealthy rich with an all-female cast. It was a tremendous hit on Broadway and was twice made into a movie, both of which were highly successful. Frustrated by masculine prejudice, she turned the situation into a highly effective demonstration of female ability.

The many years I have been involved in public speaking have taught me about the art of debate. When I first began speaking, I was convinced of the importance of gaining the audience's attention. I saw the situation as calling for a strong frontal attack. Having won the audience over, I could continue to build their interest and so carry them along with me. It does not always work that way. I all too frequently fired off my best salvos at the beginning, only to have the opposition come in at the last and deal me some devastating blows. I have now become more generous with my opponents, giving them first opportunity to speak, taking my initial presentation at a casual pace, doing anything possible to make sure I am the last one to speak. I have discovered it is of the utmost importance that I should have the last rather than the first word.

What it has taken so long for me to learn wives have known for years. They have become adept at having the last word. Superwife was certainly a woman with the last word. Thirty chapters of the book of Proverbs, wherein the writers have paraded all the traditional Jewish views of women, stressing their weaknesses, have come and gone. Now in the concluding twenty-three verses superwife has not only nullified all the negative images but has replaced them with the portrayal of a remarkable woman. The contrast between these two pictures of womanhood is stark and clear. One translation of the opening verse of chapter 31 is, "The words of King Lemuel, the *burden* that his mother taught him." The king's mother had a burden weighing heavily upon her that she must present another picture of woman that will counteract many of the traditional and widely accepted ideas of womanhood.

COMPARISONS OF VIEWS OF WOMEN

"These girls have abandoned their husbands" [Prov. 2:17].

"She will not hinder him [her husband] but help him all her life" [Prov. 31:12].

"She leads you down to death and hell" [Prov. 5:5].

"She is worth more than precious gems" [Prov. 31:10].

"She sits at the door of her house" [Prov. 9:14].

"She watches carefully all that goes on throughout her household and is never lazy" [Prov. 31:27].

"A beautiful woman lacking discretion and modesty" [Prov. 11:22].

"A woman who fears and reverences God shall be greatly praised" [Prov. 31:30].

"A nagging wife annoys like constant dripping" [Prov. 19:13].

"When she speaks her words are wise" [Prov. 31:26].

"Things that make the earth tremble—a bitter woman who when she finally marries" [Prov. 30:21].

"Kindness is the rule for everything she does" [Prov. 31:26].

"Living with a crabby woman in a lovely house" [Prov. 21:9].

"She will richly supply his needs" [Prov. 31:11].

"Come on, let us take our fill of love until morning for my husband is gone on a long trip" [Prov. 7:18–19].

"Her husband can trust her" [Prov. 31:11].

"Don't lust for their beauty" [Prov. 6.25].

"Beauty doesn't last" [Prov. 31:30].

"She that maketh ashamed is as rottenness in his bones" [Prov. 12:4].

"He praises her with these words, 'there are many fine women in the world, but you are the best of them all' " [Prov. 31:29].

Any discussion about superwife is bound to raise the issue of whether she is really a personality or is just an ideal woman, a picture concocted to be an example. In either case, she certainly represents the values wives have stood by across the centuries.

I have long realized that inquiring about someone's occupation is one of the best ways to stimulate conversation. When I was introduced to Mr. Montrose, a rather quiet man, and my hostess rushed off to greet some new arrivals, I immediately fell back on my old standby, "And what do you do for a living?" Mr. Montrose responded in a low voice, "I have my own business; I am a manufacturer." I hesitated. Once when I had pushed a question like this, I discovered my companion built caskets. Nevertheless, I pressed on and asked, "And what do you manufacture?" "Grade markers." For a moment I felt as if I were back in the undertaking business, but further inquiry revealed his company manufactured little plastic flags that fit on the top of those wooden stakes engineers drive into the roadbed during construction to indicate the desired level of the road. Because of their flexibility, the markers can be walked on by workmen's boots, run over by automobiles, and even crushed by road rollers. With an amazing flexibility, they pop back up to make certain the grade level will not be lost.

Look at what we have done to women over the years. It began in the Garden of Eden when Adam blamed Eve for his fall, forcing her into a sexual role. We have blamed women for the sexual ills that came upon our society; invading armies have slain their husbands and subjected them to rape. We have denied women an education, insisting their place is in the home and they are fit for little more than bearing children. When we have let them work, we have paid them less than men for the same work. We have refused to let them vote and barred them from some professions, notably the church. As Florence Nightingale said, "I would have given the church my hand, my head, my life but she told me to go home and do crochet in my mother's drawing room." The sexual discrimination that has been exercised against women would make the most bigoted racist look unbiased.

And through it all, these women have been like the humble grade markers in the highway. There they are, standing bravely in place, indicating the levels of life. They are the custodians of our values. We can ignore them, roll over them, or cover them; but they spring back from all the ignominies we have heaped upon them. Superwife, their representative, surely deserves to be praised by the leaders of the nation.

I had often heard stories of men who in their later years develop interests outside the home, but it never even crossed my mind that my husband would have such wayward ideas. It all happened so simply. He came home talking about this unusual woman he had met. He said she was older but had lived such a varied life and been part of so many unusual enterprises that she had a remarkable story to tell. Moreover, he piqued my curiosity by saying that in many ways she reminded him of me, "Not as pretty, of course, but that same zest for life." He assured me I would love her.

We invited her to our home. She certainly impressed me and in no time I was spending much time with her. Let me make it clear she did not push her way into our home; we were constantly inviting her. Then it happened. My husband suggested she just move in and live with us, and I agreed. She proved to be a charming guest. So good, in fact, that John was forever talking about her. It naturally followed that when we both made our platform appearances, John suggested a lecture on our houseguest's fascinating life story. One thing led to another, and we were shortly involved in weekly presentations all over the country.

My husband is a marriage counselor and an authority on home and family life, and some people think it strange we should spend so much time talking about another woman. Now he has written a book about her; and women sometimes make such snide remarks as, "It must be interesting to have another woman living so closely with you." I am compelled to admit I not only do not mind but am highly delighted to have this triangular relationship.

I once watched an interview with Will and Ariel Durant, the writers of The Story of Civilization. *As they discussed the way they worked on writing their books, Mrs. Durant said her husband falls in love with every women he writes about. I am afraid my John has done just that because he has spent so much time with superwife.*

Superwife has become so much a part of our lives that I find myself telling my friends about "the virtuous wife" of Proverbs 31 and have a feeling that anyone who has never heard about her is a traitor to the cause of women. Superwife will forever remain a proud and honored part of our home and family.

Notes

CHAPTER 1

1. G. B. Eager, "Marriage," *The International Standard Bible Encyclopaedia,* vol. 3 (Grand Rapids, Mich.: Wm. B. Eerdmans, 1960), p. 1997.
2. Max Gunther, quoted in Joseph J. Thorndike, Jr., *The Very Rich: A History of Wealth* (New York: Crown Publishers, 1976).
3. Joseph J. Thorndike, Jr., p. 102.
4. Louise Kapp Howe, "Just A Housewife," *McCalls,* November 1975, p. 157.

CHAPTER 2

1. Otto Fenichel, *The Psychoanalytic Theory of the Neurosis* (New York: W. W. Norton, 1945), p. 391.
2. A. H. Maslow, "A Dynamic Theory of Human Motivation," in Charles L. Stacey, Manfred F. De Martino, ed., *Understanding Human Motivation* (Cleveland: Howard Allen, 1958), pp. 26–47.
3. Ibid.
4. Suzanne K. Steinmetz & Murray Straus, "The Family As Cradle of Violence," *Readings in Marriage & Family 78/79* (Guilford, Conn.: Dushkin Publishing Group, 1978), p. 136.
5. Ibid. p. 135.
6. Alvin Toffler, *Future Shock* (New York: Random House, 1970).
7. James J. Lynch, *The Broken Heart* (New York: Basic Books, 1977), p. 103.
8. Pitirim Sorokin, *Leaves From a Russian Diary* (Boston: Beacon Press, 1950), p. 310.
9. Russel C. Prohl, *Woman in the Church* (Grand Rapids, Mich.: Wm. B. Eerdmans, 1957), pp. 77–78.
10. Maslow, Stacey & DeMartino, eds., *Understanding Human Motivation,* p. 38.

CHAPTER 3

1. John Telford, *The Letters of John Wesley* (London: Epworth Press, 1931), p. 322.

CHAPTER 6

1. Myra Marx Ferree, "The Confused American Housewife," *Psychology Today,* September 1976, p. 6.
2. "Wages for Housework," *McCalls,* June 1977, p. 87.
3. "Wife's Worth Hard to Appraise," Fort Worth *Star Telegram,* May 26, 1977, p. E1.
4. Frank Gilbreth, *Cheaper by the Dozen* (New York: Thomas Crowell, 1948).

CHAPTER 7

1. Elvenia Slosson, *Pioneer American Gardening* (New York: Coward, McCann, 1951), p. 252.
2. Buckner Hollingsworth, *Her Garden Was Her Delight* (New York: The Macmillan Company, 1962), p. 67.
3. "The Executive Gardener," *Business Week,* May 2, 1977, p. 87.
4. Roland Bainton, *Here I Stand* (New York: Abingdon, 1951), p. 292.
5. Alfred Lord Tennyson, "Flower in the Crannied Wall," *The Treasury of Religious Verse,* comp. Donald T. Kauffman (Westwood, N.J.: Fleming H. Revell, 1962), p. 11.
6. Elizabeth Barrett Browning, "Glory in the Commonplace," *The Treasury of Religious Verse,* p. 11.
7. *The Works of John Wesley,* vol. 8 (London: Wesleyan-Methodist Book Room, 1831), p. 35.

CHAPTER 8

1. "Iron Woman," *Newsweek,* May 23, 1977, p. 73.
2. Abraham A. Low, *Mental Health Through Will Training* (Boston: The Christopher Publishing House, 1950), p. 63.
3. Charles W. Colson, *Born Again* (Old Tappan, N.J.: Fleming H. Revell, 1976), p. 287.
4. "Ready Set Sweat," *Time,* June 6, 1977, p. 86.
5. Ibid.
6. Ibid.
7. Dale Carnegie, *Effective Speaking* (New York: Association Press, 1962), p. 40.
8. Ibid., p. 41.

CHAPTER 9

1. Roland Bainton, *Here I Stand* (New York: Abingdon Press, 1951), p. 292.
2. Ibid.
3. John Telford, *The Life of John Wesley* (London: The Epworth Press, 1947), p. 18.

CHAPTER 10

1. Dror Wertheimer, "Family Therapy Training in Israel," *Journal of Marriage and Family Counseling* 4 (April 1978), p. 83.
2. "Saints Among Us," *Time*, December 29, 1975, p. 47.
3. Ibid., p. 48.

CHAPTER 11

1. Sidney M. Jourard, *The Transparent Self* (New York: D. Van Nostrand Company, 1971), p. 108.
2. Lynch, p. 48.
3. Lynch, p. 168.
4. Jane Howard, *Families* (New York: Simon & Schuster, 1978), p. 190.

CHAPTER 12

1. Gordon W. Allport, *Personality: A Psychological Interpretation* (New York: Henry Holt and Company, 1937), p. 219.

CHAPTER 13

1. *Time*, September 12, 1977, p. 41.
2. Margaret Harmon, *Psycho-Decorating* (New York: Wyden Books, 1977).

CHAPTER 14

1. S. Pierce Carey, *William Carey* (London: Hodder and Stoughton, 1924), p. 271.
2. Lowell Thomas, *Good Evening Everybody* (New York: William Morrow and Company, 1976), p. 247.
3. James Orr, ed., *The New International Standard Bible Encyclopedia*, vol. 2 (Grand Rapids, Mich.: Wm. B. Eerdmans, 1960), p. 1109.
4. "The Inexpressive American Male: A Tragedy of American Society," in *Readings in Marriage & Family 78/79* (Sluice Dock: The Dushkin Publishing House, 1978).

CHAPTER 15

1. Sir Winston Churchill, *Great War Speeches* (London: Transworld Publishers, n.d.), p. 209.

CHAPTER 16

1. Lowell Thomas, p. 300.
2. Churchill, p. 64.

3. George Michaelson, "Maggie Kuhn: Gray Panther on the Prowl," *Parade,* October 9, 1977, p. 7.
4. Michaelson, p. 8.
5. Lynch, p. 7.
6. Lynch, p. 31.
7. Lynch, p. 38.
8. Daniel J. Leithauser, *Early Ambulation* (Springfield, Miss.: Charles C. Thomas, 1946), p. 7.
9. Kenneth Cooper, *Aerobics* (New York: M. Evans & Co., 1968), p. 102.
10. Cooper, p. 101.

CHAPTER 17

1. Norman R. Jaffray, "Good Listener," *Saturday Evening Post,* December 8, 1958, p. 40.

CHAPTER 18

1. William Barclay, *Ethics in a Permissive Society* (London: Collins, 1971), p. 56.
2. Albert Bandura, *Principles of Behavior Modification* (New York: Holt, Rinehart & Winston, 1969), p. 146.

CHAPTER 19

1. Donald R. Grant, "Dish Drying and Lessons from Mother," *Western Recorder,* August 24, 1977, p. 3.
2. John A. Newton, *Susanna Wesley and the Puritan Tradition in Methodism* (London: Epworth Press, 1968), p. 97.
3. Ibid., p. 100.
4. Rebecca Lamar Harmon, *Susanna: Mother of the Wesleys* (New York: Abingdon Press, 1968), p. 44.
5. Nehemiah Curnock, ed., *The Journal of Rev. John Wesley* (London: Epworth Press, 1960), pp. 38–39.
6. Ibid., p. 34.
7. Ibid., p. 38.
8. Harmon, p. 56.
9. Curnock, p. 33.
10. Harmon, p. 154.
11. Ibid., p. 160.
12. Ibid., p. 64.

CHAPTER 20

1. Nardi Reeder Campion, "Ask, Don't Tell," *Reader's Digest,* August 1966, p. 51.

CHAPTER 21

1. William H. Lazareth, *Luther on the Christian Home* (Philadelphia: Muhlenberg Press, 1960), p. 226.